AI

Programming for Kids

Kris Jamsa, PhD², MBA

Jamsa Media Group

Copyright 2024 Jamsa Media Group, All rights reserved.

Dedication

To Matthew Marsh,

For helping me bring AI to life.

Brief Contents

Detailed Contents

About the Author

Dr. Kris Jamsa wrote his first computer program in Algol, using punched cards, while attending the United States Air Force Academy. Since then, he has spent his career wrangling data and programs that use it.

Jamsa has a Ph.D. in Computer Science, a second Ph.D. in Education and master's degrees in computer science, Information Security, Project Management, Education, and Business. He is the author of 121 books on all aspects of programming and computing.

Kris lives with his wife, Debbie, on their ranch in Prescott, Arizona. When he is not in front of a computer screen, you can find him spending time with their horses and dogs.

Chapter 1
Getting Started with AI

Artificial intelligence, which we simply call "AI" is the process of using computer software to create programs that exhibit the ability to perform operations that normally require human intelligence, such as thinking, understanding, and responding. AI is all around us. We have self-driving cars that use AI. We can use AI to generate images from a description we provide. Search engines such as Google and Bing use AI when we ask them questions. NetFlix uses AI to recommend movies we might like and, of course, Amazon uses AI to help us find products to buy!

AI can solve many problems. In this book, we will use several different AI capabilities:

- Text generation
- Image generation
- Computer vision which lets AI tell you whats in a photo
- Natural-language processing which lets AI understand and process written and spoken words
- Speech generation which lets AI create speech from a text description
- Speech transcription which lets AI transcribe (create words for) spoken speech

In this chapter, you will use two popular AI programs, ChatGPT and Microsoft Bing Image Creator to get started with AI. We'll begin with ChatGPT.

Asking Questions to ChatGPT

ChatGPT is an AI program we can interact with to get answers to our questions and more. Let's look at some examples:

You
How would you describe AI to someone who is not technical?

 ChatGPT
Artificial Intelligence (AI) is like a smart assistant that learns and makes decisions similar to how humans do, but it's powered by computers instead of brains. It's a technology that enables machines to understand, learn from experiences, and solve problems without being explicitly programmed for each task. Imagine it as a helpful tool that can analyze information, recognize patterns, and make decisions to assist us in various ways, such as suggesting movies based on our preferences, helping doctors analyze medical images, or even guiding self-driving cars to navigate safely. AI aims to make machines smarter, enabling them to perform tasks that usually require human intelligence, making our lives easier and more efficient.

 You
I'm bored. Tell me 4 things to do.

 ChatGPT
Absolutely! Here are four diverse suggestions to help alleviate boredom:

1. **Create a Vision Board:** Collect magazines, images, quotes, and materials that represent your goals, dreams, and aspirations. Craft a vision board that visually encapsulates what you wish to achieve or manifest in the coming year. This activity not only engages your creativity but also provides focus and motivation.
2. **Try a New Recipe:** Experiment with cooking or baking by trying a new recipe. It could be a dish from a cuisine you've never attempted before or a dessert that caught your eye. Cooking offers an opportunity for creativity and can be a delicious way to spend time.
3. **Start a DIY Project:** Find a DIY project that interests you, whether it's refurbishing old furniture, creating handmade crafts, or building something from scratch. Engaging in hands-on projects can be both rewarding and fulfilling.
4. **Explore a New Podcast or Book:** Dive into a captivating podcast series or start reading a book on a topic that intrigues you. Whether it's fiction, self-help, mystery, or science fiction, getting lost in a good story or learning something new can be an excellent way to beat boredom.

You

How do I say "I am an AI programmer." in Spanish?

ChatGPT

"I am an AI programmer" in Spanish is: "Soy un programador de inteligencia artificial."

You

What is the area of a circle with a radius of 5 feet?

ChatGPT

The formula to calculate the area of a circle is given by:

$$\text{Area} = \pi \times \text{radius}^2$$

Given the radius $r = 5$ feet, we can substitute it into the formula to find the area:

$$\text{Area} = \pi \times (5\,\text{feet})^2$$

$$\text{Area} = \pi \times 25\,\text{feet}^2$$

Using the approximation for π as 3.14159, we can calculate the area:

$$\text{Area} \approx 3.14159 \times 25\,\text{feet}^2$$

$$\text{Area} \approx 78.54\,\text{square feet}$$

Therefore, the area of a circle with a radius of 5 feet is approximately 78.54 square feet.

You

Write a two verse poem about AI as Shakespeare would.

ChatGPT

Upon the woven threads of code, a mind,
Artificial intelligence, a marvel to find.
A tapestry of ones and zeros, it weaves,
In bytes and bits, its craft deceives.

Its circuits pulse with thought's allure,
A silicon soul, in data pure.
With wits unmatched, yet by man designed,
AI, a creation of the human mind.

To get started with ChatGPT, go to the OpenAI web site at **OpenAI.com** and click on the menu, as shown in Figure 1.1.

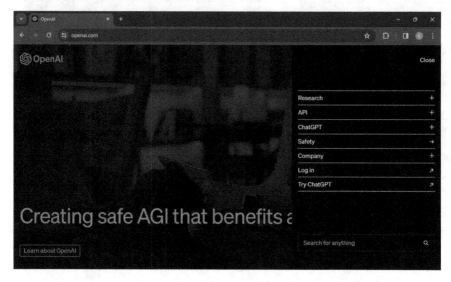

Figure 1.1: Getting started with ChatGPT at the OpenAI Web site.

Next, click on the Try ChatGPT option. The OpenAI Web site will display a page asking you to create an account. If you are 13 or older, you can create an account. If you are younger than 13, you will need to have your parents create an account. After you create your account, login. OpenAI will display the ChatGPT prompt which you can use to start asking questions, as shown in Figure 1.2.

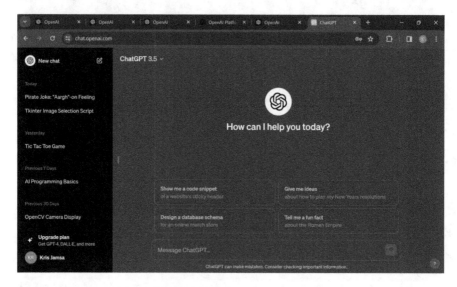

Figure 1.2: Interacting with ChatGPT.

Prompt Engineering: Asking Specific Questions

When you interact with ChatGPT the more specific you can be with your questions, the better your result will be. Computer scientists refer to the process of asking AI good questions as "prompt engineering."

Consider the following examples:

- Tell me about basketball.
- Tell me about basketball. I want to know about the NBA and WNBA.

- Write a poem.
- Write a poem about Montana and horses.

- How do I calculate the area of a circle?
- How do I calculate the area of a circle with a radius of 5?

- Write a poem.
- I am 12 years. I am trying to write a poem. Can you help me write a poem about horses.

- I'm bored.
- Today is Saturday. I have nothing to do. Can you help?

As you will learn, when you use AI to generate text or images, prompt engineering matters—meaning, the more specific you can be, the better your AI result.

Getting Your OpenAI API Key

Throughout this book, you will write programs that use OpenAI API to generate text and images. For your programs to use OpenAPI, you must have a special value called an API key. To get your API key, perform these steps:

1. Using your Web browser, go to the OpenAI Web site at **openai.com**.
2. Within the OpenAI web site, click the menu and choose Login.
3. After you login, OpenAI will display the page shown in Figure 1.3.

Figure 1.3: Selecting ChatGPT or the OpenAI API.

4. Click on the API box. OpenAI will display its API page as shown in Figure 1.4.

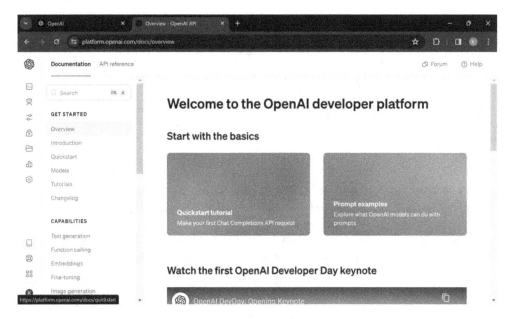

Figure 1.4: The OpenAI API page.

5. Within the page, click on the API Keys option as shown in Figure 1.5.

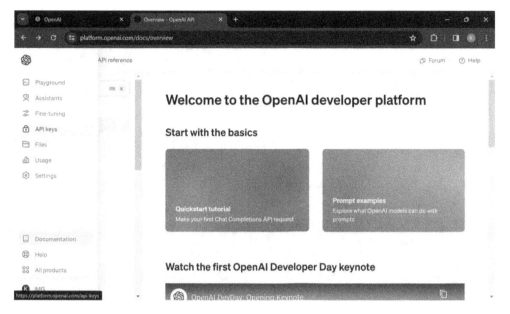

Figure 1.5: Accessing OpenAI API keys.

6. Within the API Key page, generate a key, write it down, and copy and paste it to a safe/secure file on your disk. You will need the key later when we start to program OpenAI.

To help you get started programming AI, OpenAI lets you write programs for free using your key. If you are creating many programs, you will need to pay for a key at the OpenAI site. The paid key will provide you with greater processing capabilities. As you get started, the free key should be fine.

Creating Images Using AI with Microsoft Bing Image Creator

Generating text using ChatGPT is very powerful (and fun) but creating images using AI is even better! To get started using AI-image generation, use your Web browser to go to the Microsoft Bing Image Creator Web site at **https://www.bing.com/images/create**. Your browser will display the Image Creator Web site as shown in Figure 1.6.

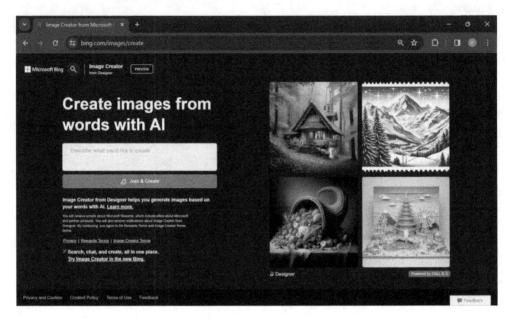

Figure 1.6: The Microsoft Bing Image Creator Web site.

Click the Join & Create button. You (or your parents) will need to create an account. After you login, Image Creator will display a page within which you can describe the image you want to create.

Within the text box, type a (detailed) description of the image you want to create. I typed: **Create a cream-colored labradoodle programming AI at a computer in a futuristic office.** Image Creator displayed the images shown in Figure 1.7.

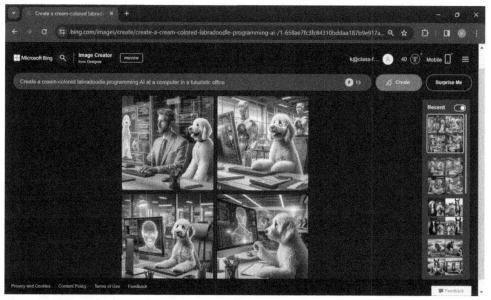

Figure 1.7 Creating images using Image Creator.

Take time to experiment with Image Creator to generate different images. Try using different prompts with less and more specifics and note your results.

Later in this book, you will learn how to create images from within your own programs.

Summary

In this chapter, you learned about artificial intelligence (AI) and how to use it to generate text and images. Specifically, you learned how to interact with ChatGPT to generate text and Microsoft Bing Image Creator to generate images. You also got your OpenAI API key which you will need to create the programs this book presents.

In the next chapter, you will set up your Python programming environment which you will use to create and run this book's programs.

Chapter 2
Setting Up Your Python Programming Environment

To create the AI programs this book presents, you will use the Python programming language—the world's most widely used programming language. In this chapter, you will set up your computer to run Python.

If you have never programmed in Python before, don't worry. You can run all the programs this book presents without any programming knowledge. If you are new to Python, you should take time to run the Python tutorial presented at the W3 Schools web site at **https://www.w3schools.com/python/** shown in Figure 2.1. The tutorial will teach you all the Python you will need to know to understand this book's programs.

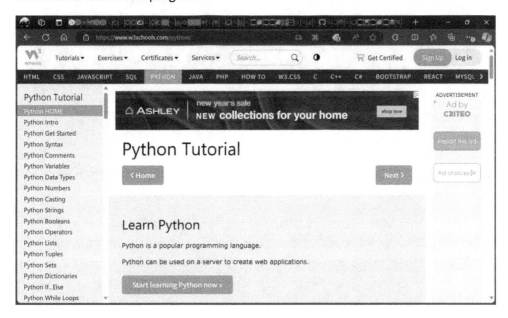

Figure 2.1: Take time to run the W3 Schools Python tutorial.

There are several different versions of Python that programmers can download and install. For this book, you should download and install Anaconda Python. As you will learn, Anaconda Python makes it very easy for you to run Python applications within an interface called a Jupyter Notebook. In fact, I've created a Jupyter Notebook that contains all this book's programs that you can download to your computer and easily run. In this way, you don't have to type the programs this book presents—the Jupyter Notebook already has them typed for you!

To install Anaconda Python, use your Web browser to go to the Web site **https://www.anaconda.com/download/** shown in Figure 2.2.

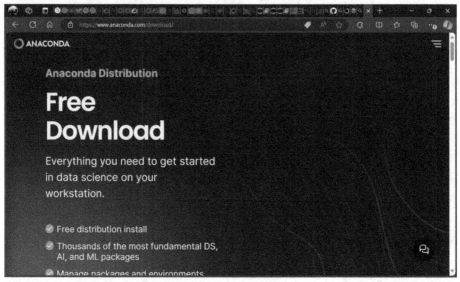

Figure 2.2: The Anaconda Python Web site.

Within the Web page, click the Download button to start the Anaconda Python installation download. Your browser should put the executable installation program within your Downloads folder. Open the Windows File Explorer and use it to select the Downloads folder. Then, double-click your mouse on the installation program to run it and install Anaconda Python.

After the Anaconda Python installation completes, select the Windows Start menu and choose All apps. Windows will display its complete Start menu. Within the Start menu, expand the Anaconda menu as shown in Figure 2.3.

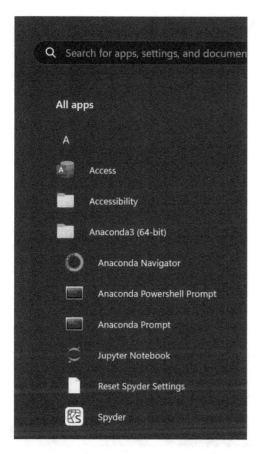

Figure 2.3: Expanding the Anaconda menu.

For now, select Jupyter Notebook menu option. Windows will open two windows—one within which it starts a notebook server and a second, similar to that shown in Figure 2.4, within which you will open a notebook which you can use to run Python programs.

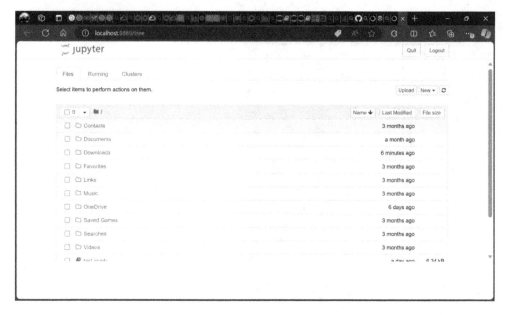

Figure 2.4: Starting Jupyter Notebook.

Within the Jupyter Notebook window, click the New button and choose Python 3 to create a new Python notebook. Your browser will open and display a new notebook as shown in Figure 2.5.

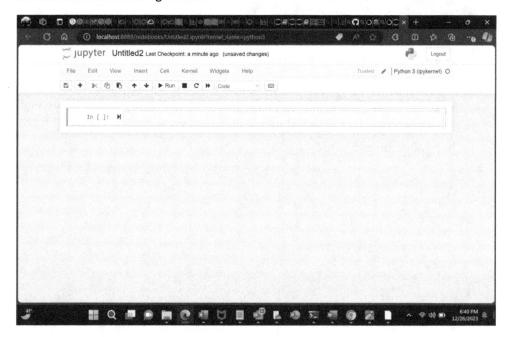

Figure 2.5: Creating a new Jupyter Notebook.

Within the Jupyter Notebook cell, type the following Python statement:

print("Hello, world")

as shown in Figure 2.6.

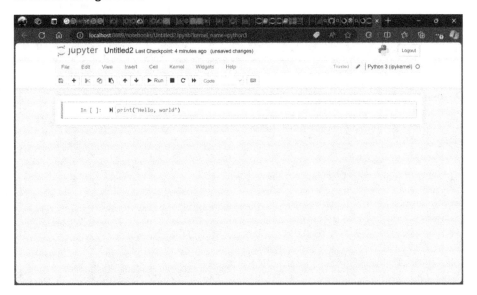

Figure 2.6: Typing a Python statement within a Jupyter Notebook cell.

Next, click the Run button to execute your statement. The notebook should display the Hello, world message as shown in Figure 2.7.

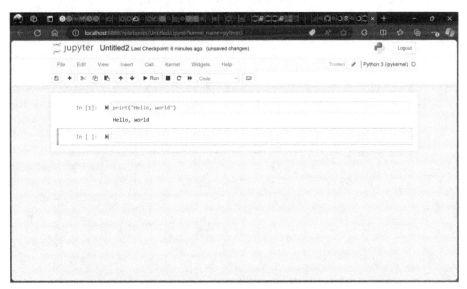

Figure 2.7: Running a Python statement within Jupyter Notebook.

Within the second notebook cell, type the following Python statements:

name = input("Type your name: ")
print("Hello ", name)

as shown in Figure 2.8.

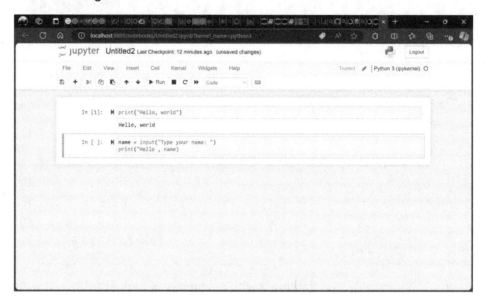

Figure 2.8: Creating a second Python program within Jupyter Notebook.

Again, click the Run button. Jupyter Notebook will execute the statements which, in turn, prompt you to enter your name as shown in Figure 2.9.

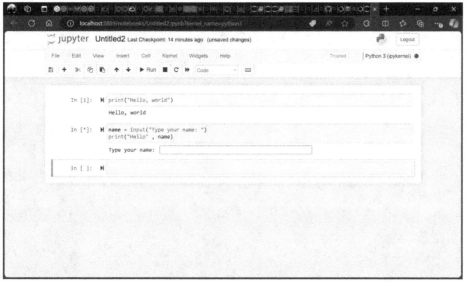

Figure 2.9: Running a program in Jupyter Notebook.

After you type your name and press Enter, the script will display a Hello message to you.

Downloading This Book's Jupyter Notebook

To make it easy for you to run the programs this book presents, I have created a Jupyter Notebook that contains the code for all the programs. To download the notebook to your computer, enter this link within your browser.

https://github.com/kjamsa/AIKids.git

Your browser will display the screen shown in Figure 2.10.

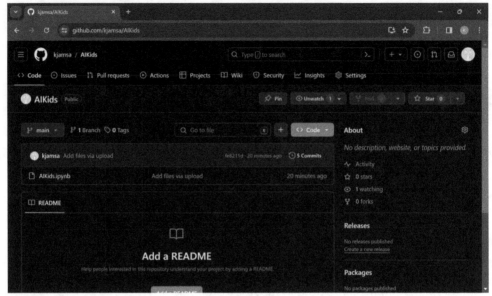

Figure 2.10: Downloading the Jupyter Notebook that contains this book's source code.

Within the page, click the AIKids.ipynb link. Github will display a page from which you can download the file to your computer. To do so, click the download button (it looks like an arrow pointing into a tray) to download the notebook file into your Downloads folder.

Next, within your Jupyter Notebook window running in your browser, select the File menu Open option. Jupyter Notebook will display the screen shown in Figure 2.11.

Figure 2.11: Opening an existing Jupyter Notebook.

Within the screen, click the Upload button. Jupyter Notebook will display an Open dialog box. Using the dialog box to go to your Downloads folder and open the file AIKids.ipynb. Jupyter Notebook will display the filename within its list of files as shown in Figure 2.12.

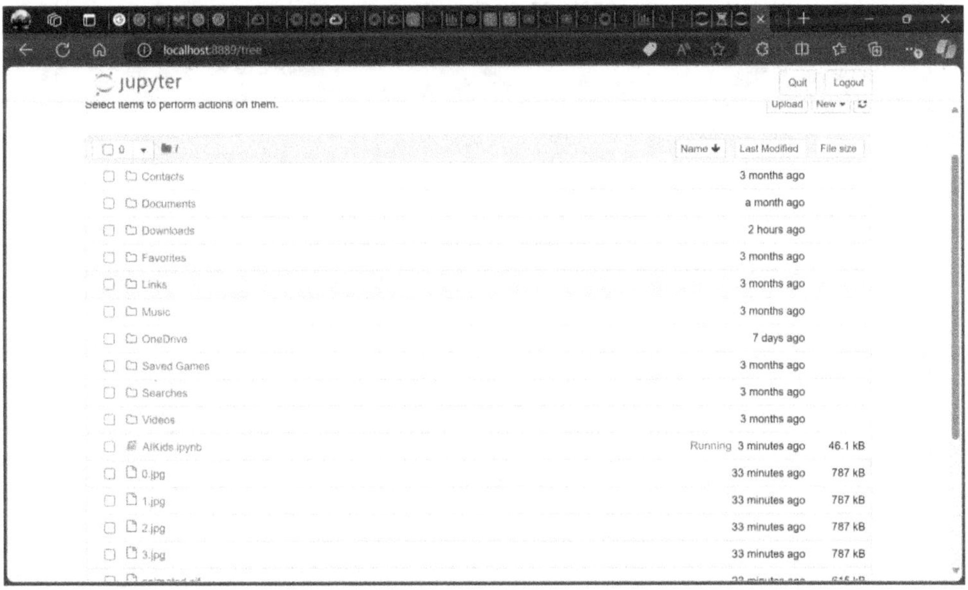

Figure 2.12: The AIKids.ipynb file.

Double click on the AIKids.ipynb file to open it within Jupyter Notebook as shown in Figure 2.13.

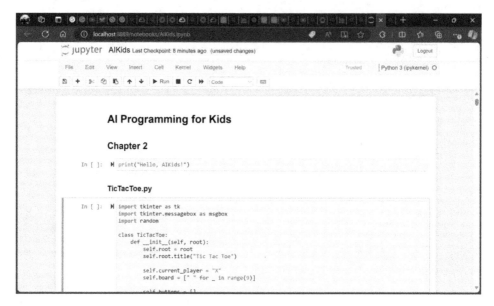

Figure 2.13: The AIKids Jupyter Notebook.

The AIKids notebook contains all the programs the book presents, organized by chapter. Click on the first cell code and click the Run button. Jupyter Notebook will display a Hello, AIKids message as shown in Figure 2.14.

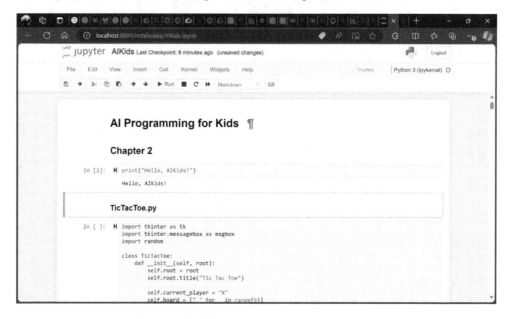

Figure 2.14: Running the AIKids hello script.

The second script for Chapter 1 is an interactive tic-tac-toe game. Click on the code's cell and click Run. Jupyter Notebook will run the interactive game, as shown in Figure 2.15.

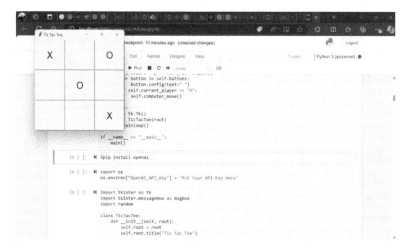

Figure 2.15: Running a tic-tac-toe application within Jupyter Notebook.

If you can successfully run the tic-tac-toe application, you are ready to move on to Chapter 3 and your first AI programs!

Preparing to Use this Book's OpenAI Programs

Following the tic-tac-toe application within your Jupyter Notebook, you will find two scripts you must run before you can run the applications this book presents, as shown in Figure 2.16.

Figure 2.16: Scripts to run before you can run this book's programs.

The first script uses the pip command to install the openai package which contains behind-the-scenes code your programs will use to interact with the OpenAI API. Click on the cell and click Run.

The second script creates an operating-system environment entry which will hold your OpenAI API key discussed in Chapter 1. Replace the text "Put Your API Key Here" with the OpenAI API key you created in Chapter 1. Then, click the Run button to run the code. You should then be set for the Chapter 3 programs!

Note: Should you close the window that contains your AIKids Jupyter notebook, you can perform these steps to resume your work.

1. Click the Windows Start menu and choose All apps.
2. Within the Windows Start menu, expand the Anaconda menu and choose Jupyter Notebook.
3. Within the Jupyter Notebook window, double click on the AIKids.ipynb file. Jupyter Notebook will open the notebook.
4. Within the notebook, find the cell just discussed that sets the operating-system environment variable for your API key and click Run.
5. You are now ready to resume where you left off in the notebook code.

Summary

In this chapter, you installed Anaconda Python and ran Python code within your first Jupyter Notebook. You then downloaded to your computer the Jupyter Notebook that contains all the programs for this book.

To get started, you ran a tic-tac-toe program. After that, you ran a script that will make your OpenAI API key available to all this book's programs.

Chapter 3
Generating Text Using AI

The GPT in ChatGPT stands for Generative Pretrained Transformer. It is a complex mathematical model that allows it to represent text, generate text, understand text, and process text, much like the human brain does.

Most users are familiar with ChatGPT's text generation and processing capabilities by interacting with it using the ChatGPT prompt. Here's a few examples:

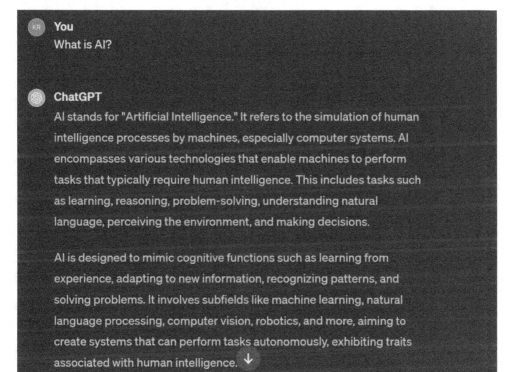

You
In one paragraph, define AI text generation

ChatGPT
AI text generation involves the utilization of artificial intelligence technologies, particularly machine learning algorithms and deep neural networks, to autonomously create coherent and contextually relevant textual content resembling human language. These models are trained on extensive datasets of human-generated text, allowing them to learn linguistic patterns, semantics, and syntactic structures. Leveraging this acquired knowledge, AI text generation systems generate new text by predicting and assembling words, phrases, and sentences based on the context or input provided, producing a wide array of content types such as articles, stories, code snippets, customer support responses, and more, catering to diverse applications across industries and domains.

You
Write me a three verse poem about Montana and horses.

ChatGPT
In Montana's embrace, wild horizons roam,
Where prairies meet skies, a boundless home,
Hooves drum the earth in a rhythmic score,
Horses gallop free, their spirits soar.

Across vast plains, where nature reigns supreme,
Majestic stallions and mares roam the dream,
Their mane's dance with the winds' gentle force,
Graceful companions on Montana's course.

In Montana's heart, where the rugged land meets,
Horses run free, in unison, their beats,
Their beauty untamed, a sight to behold,
In Montana's tale, their stories are told.

You
List 10 ways to use text generation

 ChatGPT
Certainly! Here are ten ways text generation can be applied across various fields and purposes:

1. **Content Creation:** Generating blog posts, articles, product descriptions, and social media content to engage audiences and drive traffic.
2. **Language Translation:** Automating the translation of text between languages to aid communication and accessibility.
3. **Customer Support:** Providing automated responses to customer queries through chatbots or automated email responses.
4. **Coding Assistance:** Generating code snippets, documentation, or explanations to assist developers and programmers.
5. **Creative Writing:** Assisting writers by generating prompts, story outlines, or even entire narratives.
6. **Personalized Messaging:** Crafting personalized messages for marketing, emails, or greetings based on user data.
7. **Data Augmentation:** Expanding datasets for machine learning models by generating additional text samples for training.
8. **Summarization:** Automatically generating summaries of articles, research papers, or lengthy documents.
9. **Poetry and Lyrics:** Creating poetry or song lyrics based on given themes, styles, or patterns.
10. **Educational Aids:** Generating study guides, quizzes, or learning materials for educational purposes.

As you have learned, by providing ChatGPT with good prompts, you can use it to get very detailed information on a wide range of topics.

In this chapter, you will learn how to use OpenAI and ChatGPT to generate and process text within your own programs.

Creating Quick Text Generation with Your Own Program

Ideally, you will run this chapter's programs from within the AIKids Jupyter Notebook, as discussed in Chapter 2. That is by far the easiest way to run this book's programs.

That said, you can, instead, run the programs from an Anaconda system prompt. To do so, you need to create a simple application for creating images. You can do that by starting the Windows Notepad accessory and typing the following program. You can also download the program from my Web site, copy and paste the code to the Windows Notepad, and save the file as SimpleText.py using your editor.

http://www.class-files.com/SimpleText.html

Before you can run this program from the Anaconda prompt, you must have an OpenAI API key as discussed in Chapter 1. Then, from the system prompt, you must issue the following SET command that creates an entry in operating system that will remember the key:

C:\AIKids> SET OPEN_API_KEY=put your key here <Enter>

When your script runs, it will ask the operating system for your key value. In this way, you don't hard code your key into your Python scripts where others could see, and possibly later use it.

The following code implements SimpleText.py:

```python
from openai import OpenAI
import os

key = os.getenv('OpenAI_API_Key')

# Set your OpenAI API key here
client = OpenAI(api_key = key)

# Set the prompt for ChatGPT
prompt_text = "Tell me 10 things I should know about AI."

# Call the ChatGPT model
response = client.chat.completions.create(
  model="gpt-4",
  messages=[
   {"role": "user", "content": prompt_text}
  ]
)

print(response.choices[0].message.content)
```

When you run the script, it will ask OpenAI to generate text for 10 things you should know about AI. After ChatGPT generates the list, the script will display the following output:

C:\AIKids> python SimpleText.py <Enter>

1. AI stands for Artificial Intelligence: It refers to machines or software that exhibit capabilities which mimic or replicate human intelligence.

2. AI can learn and adapt: Through machine learning, AI can learn from data and improve its execution of tasks over time, adjusting to new inputs and improving its predictive accuracy.

3. AI is not new: Even though it feels like a modern development, the concept of AI has been around since ancient times, with Greek myths of automatons. However, AI as a field of research was officially founded in 1956.

4. There are two types of AI: Narrow AI, which is designed to perform a single task, such as voice recognition, and General AI, which will be able to outperform humans at most economically valuable work. However, General AI is currently theoretical and does not exist.

5. AI can be found in daily use: From Google search to Siri to Alexa to Netflix recommendations - all these services use AI.

6. AI has the potential to revolutionize industries: From manufacturing and healthcare to finance and transportation, AI can significantly revamp operations and provide unprecedented efficiency.

7. Ethical and societal impact: AI usage can lead to job displacements and also raises privacy and data handling concerns. It also presents ethical quandaries in areas like AI in warfare or decision-making AI applications.

8. AI relies on data: AI systems learn and improve by processing large amounts of data. The more data the system is fed, the more accurate its outputs.

9. AI is not infallible: Even though AI systems can reach high accuracy levels, they can still make mistakes. These mistakes can stem from inaccurate data, coding errors or a lack of ability to understand complex human emotions and thoughts.

10. AI is constantly evolving: The field of AI is continuously advancing, with newer techniques, concepts, and applications emerging regularly. For instance,

Reinforcement Learning and Quantum Computing are some of the latest advancements in the AI domain.

To direct ChatGPT to generate text for a different topic, edit the script and change the line that uses the prompt_text variable to describe the text you desire (you can also make this change in the Jupyter Notebook code):

prompt_text = "Tell me 10 things I should know about AI."

Save your program and run it again. This time, Python will display the newly generated text for your topic.

For example, assume you change the text to:

prompt_text = "Write a two paragraph summary on the history of basketball."

When you run the script, Python will display the following output:

C:\AIKids> python SimpleText.py   <Enter>
Basketball was invented in December 1891 by the Canadian clergyman, educator, and physician James Naismith. Naismith introduced the game when he was an instructor at the International YMCA Training School in Springfield, Massachusetts. He was asked to create a new game to entertain his students indoors during the winter and keep his track and field runners fit. He conceived the sport within a couple of weeks and wrote down the basic rules, encompassed in 13 key points, outlining the method of play. The initial games used a soccer ball and two peach baskets as goals; hence the sport's name.

The first public match of basketball took place in Springfield on March 11, 1892. By the early 20th century, basketball had spread across the United States and Canada via YMCA networks, colleges, and high schools. In 1936, it was included in the Berlin Olympic Games as an official competitive sport. In 1949, The National Basketball Association (NBA) was founded in the United States, which helped popularize basketball on a global scale. Over the years, basketball has evolved with changes to rules and advancements in equipment, becoming the sport we know today.

Let's understand the code. The first two lines import the Python packages the code will use for OpenAI and to get your API key from the operating system:

from openai import OpenAI
import os

The next line gets your API key from the operating system so you don't hard code your key into your code where other people could see it:

key = os.getenv('OpenAI_API_Key')

The next few lines set up OpenAI and then call the OpenAI API to generate the text. After OpenAI is done, the script displays the generated text:

```
# Set the prompt for ChatGPT
prompt_text = "Tell me 10 things I should know about AI."

# Call the ChatGPT model
response = client.chat.completions.create(
  model="gpt-4",
  messages=[
   {"role": "user", "content": prompt_text}
  ]
)

print(response.choices[0].message.content)
```

Getting the ChatGPT Text Prompt from the User

The previous program worked—it generated our desired text. But each time you want to generate different text, you have to change the program. A better program would ask the user for text they want ChatGPT to generate. To ask the user for the text, you can use the following statement:

prompt_text = input("Describe the text you want ChatGPT to generate: ")

In this case, the input function will display a prompt on the screen for the user to enter the text they desire. It will then assign whatever the user types to the variable prompt_text.

You can download the code for AskText.py from my Web site at **http://www.class-files.com/AskText.html**.

Using your text editor, create the following Python script, AskText.py, which asks the user for their text description:

from openai import OpenAI

```
import os

key = os.getenv('OpenAI_API_Key')

# Set your OpenAI API key here
client = OpenAI(api_key = key)

# Set the prompt for ChatGPT
prompt_text = input("Describe the text you want ChatGPT to generate: ")

# Call the ChatGPT model
response = client.chat.completions.create(
  model="gpt-4",
  messages=[
   {"role": "user", "content": prompt_text}
  ]
)

print(response.choices[0].message.content)
```

When you run the script, Python will display the following output:

C:\AIKids> python AskImage.py <Enter>
Describe the text you want ChatGPT to generate:

After you type your text and press Enter, the script will generate your desired results.

Creating a Fancy Text-Generation Program

The previous two text-generation programs created the desired text. The second program, AskText.py, improved on the first by using the input function to get the desired text from the user. The following Python script, Text.py, creates a fancier user interface, similar to that shown in Figure 3.1.

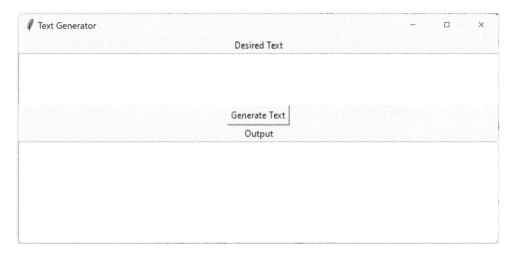

Figure 3.1: Prompting the user for a description of the text they want to create.

After the user describes the text and clicks the Generate Text button, the script will display the image as shown in Figure 3.2.

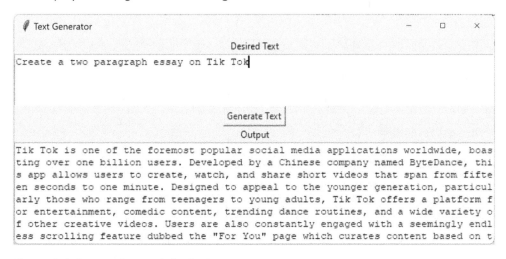

Figure 3.2 Generating and displaying text.

Take time to experiment with the application. Ask it to create a poem, song, or story.

Again, you can run this program using Jupiter Notebook or you can download the code from **http://www.class-files.com/Text.htm**l.

The following code implements the Text.py script:

```
import tkinter as tk
from openai import OpenAI
```

```python
import os

key = os.getenv('OpenAI_API_Key')

# Set your OpenAI API key here
client = OpenAI(api_key = key)

def generate_text():
    output_text.delete(1.0, tk.END)  # Clear any existing text
    generate_button.config(state=tk.DISABLED)  # Disable the button

    prompt_text = desired_text.get(1.0, tk.END)

    # Call the ChatGPT model
    response = client.chat.completions.create(
      model="gpt-4",
      messages=[
        {"role": "user", "content": prompt_text}
      ]
    )

    output_text.insert(tk.END, response.choices[0].message.content)
    generate_button.config(state=tk.NORMAL)  # Enable the button

import threading

def call_api_in_thread():
    # Function to call the API in a separate thread
    thread = threading.Thread(target=generate_text)
    thread.start()

root = tk.Tk()
root.title("Text Generator")

# Create and place the label for the desired text box
desired_text_label = tk.Label(root, text="Desired Text")
desired_text_label.pack()

# Create and place the text box for the desired text
desired_text = tk.Text(root, height=4, width=80)
desired_text.pack()
```

```
# Create and place the button to generate text
generate_button = tk.Button(root, text="Generate Text",
command=call_api_in_thread)
generate_button.pack()

# Create and place the label for the output text box
output_label = tk.Label(root, text="Output")
output_label.pack()

# Create and place the second text box for the output
output_text = tk.Text(root, height=8, width=80)
output_text.pack()

root.mainloop()
```

Again, you can run this program using the AIKids Jupyter Notebook.

To run the script, use:

C:\AIKids> python Text.py <Enter>

Python will display the window previously shown in Figure 3.1, which you can use to describe your desired text.

Let's understand the code. Much of the code is similar to the first two programs you created in that it prompts ChatGPT to create images. The rest of the code builds the user interface that appears in the window.

The first three lines of the code tell Python which packages our program will use:

```
import tkinter as tk
from openai import OpenAI
import os
```

Next, the program gets your API key which it will use to call the OpenAI API and uses the key to prepare OpenAI for use. By getting the API key from the operating-system environment, you do not need to hard code the key into your code which would allow others to see (and possibly use) it:

```
key = os.getenv('OpenAI_API_Key')

# Set your OpenAI API key here
client = OpenAI(api_key = key)
```

The generate_text function does most of the work:

```
def generate_text():
    output_text.delete(1.0, tk.END)  # Clear any existing text
    generate_button.config(state=tk.DISABLED)  # Disable the button

    prompt_text = desired_text.get(1.0, tk.END)

    # Call the ChatGPT model
    response = client.chat.completions.create(
      model="gpt-4",
      messages=[
        {"role": "user", "content": prompt_text}
      ]
    )

    output_text.insert(tk.END, response.choices[0].message.content)
    generate_button.config(state=tk.NORMAL)  # Enable the button
```

To start, the function deletes the contents of the Output text box, clearing it in preparation of the new output.

Then, the program disables the Generate Text button. That's because OpenAI may take some time to generate the image, so we disable the button the user can't click it again while OpenAI is working.

Next, the function gets the contents of the Desired Text text box and assigns it to the prompt that the function will pass to the OpenAI API:

```
prompt_text = desired_text.get(1.0, tk.END)
```

The function then calls the OpenAI API, telling it to use the GPT-4 model and passing to the API the user's prompt text. After OpenAI generates the text, the function will assign the generated text to the Output text box.

The function then re-enables the Generate Text button.

When your programs call the OpenAI AI to generate text (or images and speech) OpenAI may take some time to generate the result. When we call OpenAI from a script that uses tkinter to display a window, this delay can cause problems with our user interface. To eliminate these problems, we'll create a second thread in our script that asks OpenAI to generate the text, while our program's main thread continues to manage our user interface. To create the second thread, we'll use Python's threading package (which we import) and we'll create a second thread to call our generate_text function which interacts with OpenAI:

```
import threading

def call_api_in_thread():
    # Function to call the API in a separate thread
    thread = threading.Thread(target=generate_text)
    thread.start()
```

Finally, the rest of our code creates the original user interface that lets the user describe the image they desire. Do not worry too much yet, about the code that builds the user interface. The statements are basic tkinter operations, several of which we will discuss throughout this book.

When the user clicks the Generate Text button, the code will call our function call_api_in_thread which, in turn, calls OpenAI:

```
# Create and place the button to get the joke
generate_button = tk.Button(root, text="Play Audio",
command=call_api_in_thread)
generate_button.pack()
```

Summary

In this chapter, you learned to use AI to generate text. Your first program was pretty simple, but each time you wanted to create different text, you had to edit and save the program. Your second program was better in that it used the input function to ask the user for the text they wanted to generate. Finally, in the third program, you created a fancy user interface for the script.

In the next chapter, you will learn to use OpenAI to create several applications that generate jokes about specific topics.

Chapter 4
Creating a Joke Generator

Jokes are funny. But, coming up with a joke can be hard. In this chapter, you will solve that problem by creating a program that uses AI to generate your jokes for you!

Here's a few examples:

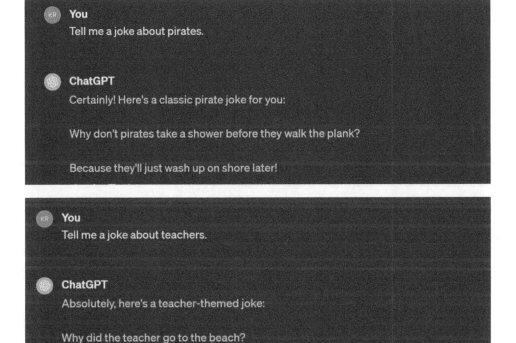

Creating a Quick Joke Generator

Again, ideally you will run this program using the AIKids Jupyter Notebook. If you are instead working from the Anaconda prompt, to create a simple joke generator, start Notepad and type the following program. Remember, you can also download the program from my Web site and save the file as SimpleJoke.py using your editor.

http://www.class-files.com/SimpleJoke.html

The following code implements SimpleJoke.py:

```
from openai import OpenAI
import os

key = os.getenv('OpenAI_API_Key')

# Set your OpenAI API key here
client = OpenAI(api_key = key)

# Set the prompt for ChatGPT
prompt_text = "Tell me a joke about football."

# Call the ChatGPT model
response = client.chat.completions.create(
  model="gpt-4",
  messages=[
   {"role": "user", "content": prompt_text}
  ]
)

print(response.choices[0].message.content)
```

When you run the program, Python will display the following output:

```
C:\AIKids> python SimpleJoke.py  <Enter>
Why don't grasshoppers watch football?

Because they prefer cricket!
```

To change your program so it tells a joke about a different topic, edit the line the line that contains the prompt_line variable. For example, to create a joke about homework, you would change the line to:

```
prompt_text = "Tell me a joke about homework."
```

Save your program and run it again. This time, Python will display the following output:

```
C:\AIKids> python SimpleJoke.py  <Enter>
Why don't we ever see homework in public?
```

Because it's always "home," working!

The code is very similar to the programs you created in Chapter 3. The first two lines import the Python packages the code will use for OpenAI and to get your API key from the operating system. The next line gets your API key from the operating system so you don't hard code your key into your code where other people could see it. The next few lines set up OpenAI and then call the OpenAI API to get the joke. After OpenAI is done, the print statement prints the joke.

Getting the Joke Topic from the User

The previous program worked—it created jokes. But each time we wanted a joke on a different topic, we had to change the program. A better program would ask the user for the joke topic and then create the joke. To ask the user for a joke topic, we can use the following statement:

joke_topic = input("For what topic do you want a joke? ")

In this case, the input function will display a prompt on the screen for the user to enter a joke topic. It will then assign whatever the user types to the variable joke_topic.

We can then build our prompt by joining together two strings:

Prompt_text = "Tell me a joke about " + joke_topic

Using your text editor, create the following Python script, AskJoke.py, which asks the user for a joke topic and then tells them a joke. You can also download the code from my Web site at **http://www.class-files.com/AskJoke.hml**.

```
from openai import OpenAI
import os

key = os.getenv('OpenAI_API_Key')

# Set your OpenAI API key here
client = OpenAI(api_key = key)

joke_topic = input("For what topic do you want a joke? ")

# Set the prompt for ChatGPT
prompt_text = "Tell me a joke about " + joke_topic
```

```
# Call the ChatGPT model
response = client.chat.completions.create(
  model="gpt-4",
  messages=[
   {"role": "user", "content": prompt_text}
  ]
)

print(response.choices[0].message.content)
```

When you run the script, Python will display the following output:

```
C:\AIKids> python AskJoke.py  <Enter>
For what topic do you want a joke? Computers
Why don't computers take their hats off?

Because they have bad 'Caps Lock.'
```

Creating a Fancy Joke Program

The previous two joke programs told us jokes. The second program, AskJoke.py, improved on the first by using the input function to get the joke topic from the user. The following Python script, Joke.py, creates a fancier user interface, similar to that shown in Figure 4.1.

Figure 4.1: Prompting the user for a joke.

After the user types their joke topic and clicks the Tell Me a Joke button, the script will call ChatGPT to get the joke, displaying the joke in a text box, as shown in Figure 4.2.

Figure 4.2: Displaying a joke within a text box.

The following code implements the Joke.py script. You can also download the code from my Web site at **http://www.class-files.com/Joke.html**.

```
import tkinter as tk
from openai import OpenAI
import os

key = os.getenv('OpenAI_API_Key')

# Set your OpenAI API key here
client = OpenAI(api_key = key)

def GetJoke():
    get_joke_button.config(state=tk.DISABLED)  # Disable the button
    joke_text.delete(1.0, tk.END)  # Clear any existing text

    prompt_text = "Tell me a joke about " + joke_topic.get()
    # Call the ChatGPT model
    response = client.chat.completions.create(
      model="gpt-4",
        messages=[
          {"role": "user", "content": prompt_text}
        ]
    )

    joke_text.insert(tk.END, response.choices[0].message.content)  # Insert the
                                    # joke into the second text box
    get_joke_button.config(state=tk.NORMAL)  # Enable the button

import threading

def call_api_in_thread():
    # Function to call the API in a separate thread
```

```
    thread = threading.Thread(target=GetJoke)
    thread.start()

root = tk.Tk()
root.title("Joke Window")

# Create and place the label for the joke topic text box
joke_topic_label = tk.Label(root, text="Joke Topic")
joke_topic_label.pack()

# Create and place the one-line text box for the joke topic
joke_topic = tk.Entry(root)
joke_topic.pack()

# Create and place the empty four-line text box
joke_text = tk.Text(root, height=4)
joke_text.pack()

# Create and place the button to get the joke
get_joke_button = tk.Button(root, text="Tell Me a Joke",
command=call_api_in_thread)
get_joke_button.pack()

root.mainloop()
```

To run the script, use:

C:\AIKids> python Joke.py <Enter>

Python will display the window previously shown in Figure 4.1, which you can use to ask for jokes.

Let's understand the code. Much of the code is similar to the first two programs you created in that it prompts ChatGPT to return a joke. The rest of the code builds the user interface that appears in the window.

The first three lines of the code tell Python which packages our program will use:

```
import tkinter as tk
from openai import OpenAI
import os
```

Next, the program gets your API key which it will use to call the OpenAI API and uses the key to prepare OpenAI for use:

```
key = os.getenv('OpenAI_API_Key')

# Set your OpenAI API key here
client = OpenAI(api_key = key)
```

The GetJoke function does most of the work:

```
def GetJoke():
  get_joke_button.config(state=tk.DISABLED)  # Disable the button
  joke_text.delete(1.0, tk.END) # Clear any existing text

  prompt_text = "Tell me a joke about " + joke_topic.get()
  # Call the ChatGPT model
  response = client.chat.completions.create(
   model="gpt-4",
    messages=[
     {"role": "user", "content": prompt_text}
    ]
  )

  joke_text.insert(tk.END, response.choices[0].message.content)  # Insert the
                                # joke into the second text box
  get_joke_button.config(state=tk.NORMAL)  # Enable the button
```

To start, the program disables the Tell Me a Joke button. That's because OpenAI may take some time to think of a joke, so we disable the button the user can't click it again while OpenAI is working.

Next, the code deletes the previous joke results from the text box so it is empty for us to display our joke within.

The line with prompt_text creates the string we will pass to OpenAI that tells it what to do. In this case, we want OpenAI to tell us a joke about the topic the user enters.

Next, we call OpenAI to get the joke. When OpenAI is done, we insert the joke into the output text box and we re-enable the button so the user can try another joke if they want.

As discussed, OpenAI may take some time to think of a joke. When we call OpenAI from a script that uses tkinter to display a window, this delay can cause problems with our user interface. To eliminate these problems, we'll create a second thread in our script that asks OpenAI the question, while our program's main thread continues to manage our user interface. To create the second thread, we'll use Python's threading package (which we import) and we'll create a second thread to call our GetJoke function which interacts with OpenAI:

```
import threading

def call_api_in_thread():
    # Function to call the API in a separate thread
    thread = threading.Thread(target=GetJoke)
    thread.start()
```

Finally, the rest of our code creates our two text boxes and the Tell Me a Joke button. Don't worry too much yet about the code that builds the user interface. We'll see other programs that do similar processing and we'll discuss each, a little bit at a time.

When the user clicks the Tell Me a Joke button, the code will call our function call_api_in_thread which, in turn, calls OpenAI:

```
# Create and place the button to get the joke
get_joke_button = tk.Button(root, text="Tell Me a Joke",
command=call_api_in_thread)
get_joke_button.pack()
```

Summary

In this chapter, you learned to use AI to generate jokes for you. Your first program was pretty simple, but each time you wanted a different joke, you had to edit and save the program. Your second program was better in that it used the input function to ask the user for the joke topic. Finally, in the third program, you created a fancy user interface for the script.

In the next chapter, you will learn to use AI to translate text from one language to another.

Chapter 5
Using AI to Translate Text

Not everyone reads and speaks English. The good news, however, is using AI, you can quickly translate text from one language to another.

Here's a few examples:

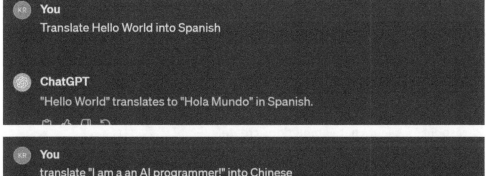

In this chapter, you will learn how to use AI to translate text from one language to another within your own programs.

Creating a Quick Language Translator

Again, you can run this program using the AIKids Jupyter Notebook. If you are working from the Anaconda prompt, to create a simple language translator, start Notepad and type the following program. Remember, you can also download the program from my Web site and save the file as SimpleTranslator.py using your editor.

http://www.class-files.com/SimpleTranslator.html

The following code implements SimpleTranslator.py:

```python
from openai import OpenAI
import os

key = os.getenv('OpenAI_API_Key')

# Set your OpenAI API key here
client = OpenAI(api_key = key)

text_to_translate = "I am an AI programmer."
language = "English"
target_language = "Spanish"

# Set the prompt for ChatGPT
prompt_text = "Translate the following text from " + language + " to " +
target_language + ":" + text_to_translate

# Call the ChatGPT model
response = client.chat.completions.create(
  model="gpt-4",
  messages=[
   {"role": "user", "content": prompt_text}
  ]
)

print(text_to_translate + " in " + target_language + " is:")
print(response.choices[0].message.content)
```

When you run the program, Python will display the following output:

C:\AIKids> python SimpleTranslator.py <Enter>
I am an AI programmer. in Spanish is:
Soy un programador de IA.

To change your program so it translates different text, edit the line the line that contains the text_to_translate variable. For example, to create a translate text about dog, you would change the line to:

text_to_translate = "I have a dog named Baxter."

Likewise, to change the target language, edit the program to change the variable target_language to the language you desire:

56

target_language = "Chinese"

Save your program and run it again. This time, Python will display the following output:

C:\AIKids> python SimpleTranslator.py <Enter>
I have a dog named Baxter. in Chinese is:
我有一只叫做Baxter的狗。

The code is very similar to the programs you created in Chapters 3 and 4. The first two lines import the Python packages the code will use for OpenAI and to get your API key from the operating system. The next line gets your API key from the operating system so you don't hard code your key into your code where other people could see it. The next few lines set up OpenAI and then call the OpenAI API to get the translation. After OpenAI is done, the print statement prints the translation.

Getting the Text and Target Language from the User

The previous program worked—it translated text. But each time you want to translate different text or use a different language, you had to change the program. A better program would ask the user for the text and target language then perform the translation. To ask the user for the text and language, we can use the following statement:

text_to_translate = input("What text do you want to translate? ")
target_language = input("What language do you desire? ")

In this case, the input function will display a prompt on the screen for the user to enter a topic. It will then assign whatever the user types to the variable text_to_translate and the language they desire into the variable target_language.

Using your text editor, create the following Python script, AskTranslatior.py, which asks the user for text and a target language. You can also download this program from my Web site at **http://www.class-files.com/AskTranslator.html**.

from openai import OpenAI
import os

key = os.getenv('OpenAI_API_Key')

```python
# Set your OpenAI API key here
client = OpenAI(api_key = key)

language = "English"
text_to_translate = input("What text do you want to translate? ")
target_language = input("What language do you desire? ")

# Set the prompt for ChatGPT
prompt_text = "Translate the following text from " + language + " to " +
target_language + ":" + text_to_translate

# Call the ChatGPT model
response = client.chat.completions.create(
  model="gpt-4",
  messages=[
   {"role": "user", "content": prompt_text}
  ]
)

print(text_to_translate + " in " + target_language + " is:")
print(response.choices[0].message.content)
```

When you run the script, Python will display the following output:

C:\AIKids> python AskTranslator.py <Enter>
What text do you want to translate? I am a great programmer!

What language do you desire? German
I am a great programmer! in German is:
Ich bin ein großartiger Programmierer!

Creating a Fancy Text-Translation Program

The previous two programs translated text. The second program, AskTranslator.py, improved on the first by using the input function to get the text and target language topic from the user. The following Python script, Translator.py, creates a fancier user interface, similar to that shown in Figure 5.1.

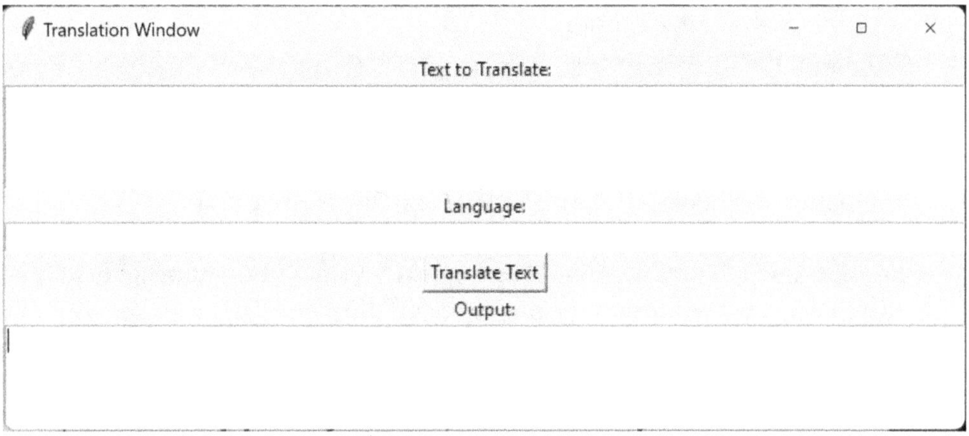

Figure 5.1: Prompting the user for text to translate.

After the user types their text, selects a language and clicks the Translate Text button, the script will call ChatGPT to get the translation displaying the result in a text box, as shown in Figure 5.2.

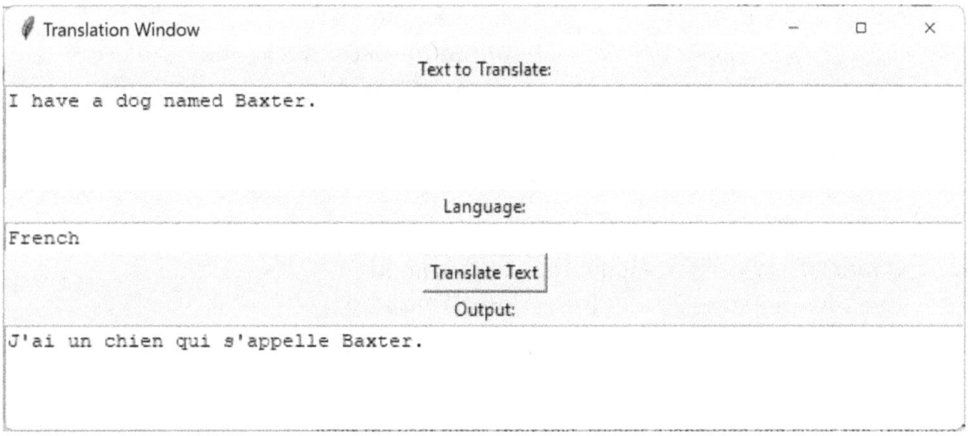

Figure 5.2: Displaying a translation within a text box.

The following code implements the Translator.py script. You can also download the code from my Web site at **http://www.class-files.com/Translator.html.**

```
import tkinter as tk
from openai import OpenAI
import os

key = os.getenv('OpenAI_API_Key')
```

```python
# Set your OpenAI API key here
client = OpenAI(api_key = key)

def GetTranslation():
    get_translation_button.config(state=tk.DISABLED)  # Disable the button
    translation_text.delete(1.0, tk.END)  # Clear any existing text

    prompt_text = "Translate the following text " + translation_topic.get('1.0',
'end-1c') + " into " + translation_language.get('1.0', 'end-1c')

    # Call the ChatGPT model
    response = client.chat.completions.create(
      model="gpt-4",
        messages=[
          {"role": "user", "content": prompt_text}
        ]
    )

    translation_text.insert(tk.END, response.choices[0].message.content)
                                    # Insert the text
                                    # into the second text box
    get_translation_button.config(state=tk.NORMAL)  # Enable the button

import threading

def call_api_in_thread():
    # Function to call the API in a separate thread
    thread = threading.Thread(target=GetTranslation)
    thread.start()

root = tk.Tk()
root.title("Translation Window")

translation_topic_label = tk.Label(root, text="Text to Translate:")
translation_topic_label.pack()
translation_topic = tk.Text(root, height=4, width=80)
translation_topic.pack()

# Create and place the empty one-line text box
language_label = tk.Label(root, text="Language:")
language_label.pack()
translation_language = tk.Text(root, height=1, width=80)
```

```
translation_language.pack()

# Create and place the button to get the joke
get_translation_button = tk.Button(root, text="Translate Text",
command=call_api_in_thread)
get_translation_button.pack()

result_label = tk.Label(root, text="Output:")
result_label.pack()
# Create and place the empty four-line text box
translation_text = tk.Text(root, height=4, width=80)
translation_text.pack()

root.mainloop()
```

Again, type the code using your text editor, or, download the code from my Web site at **http://www.class-files.com/Translator.html**.

To run the script, use:

C:\AIKids> python Translator.py <Enter>

Python will display the window previously shown in Figure 5.1, which you can use to translate text.

Let's understand the code. Much of the code is similar to the first two programs you created in that it prompts ChatGPT to translate text. The rest of the code builds the user interface that appears in the window.

The first three lines of the code tell Python which packages our program will use:

```
import tkinter as tk
from openai import OpenAI
import os
```

Next, the program gets your API key which it will use to call the OpenAI API and uses the key to prepare OpenAI for use:

```
key = os.getenv('OpenAI_API_Key')

# Set your OpenAI API key here
client = OpenAI(api_key = key)
```

The GetTranslation function does most of the work:

```
def GetTranslation():
    get_translation_button.config(state=tk.DISABLED)  # Disable the button
    translation_text.delete(1.0, tk.END)  # Clear any existing text

    prompt_text = "Translate the following text " + translation_topic.get('1.0',
'end-1c') + " into " + translation_language.get('1.0', 'end-1c')

    # Call the ChatGPT model
    response = client.chat.completions.create(
      model="gpt-4",
       messages=[
         {"role": "user", "content": prompt_text}
       ]
    )

    translation_text.insert(tk.END, response.choices[0].message.content)
                              # Insert the text
                              # into the second text box
    get_translation_button.config(state=tk.NORMAL)  # Enable the button
```

To start, the function disables the Translate Text button. That's because OpenAI may take some time to perform the translation, so we disable the button the user can't click it again while OpenAI is working.

Next, the code deletes the previous translation results from the text box so it is empty for us to display our joke within.

The line with prompt_text creates the string we will pass to OpenAI that tells it what to do. In this case, we want OpenAI to the text the user types based on the specified language.

Next, we call OpenAI to get the translation. When OpenAI is done, we insert the translation into the output text box and we re-enable the button so the user can try another translation if they want.

As discussed, OpenAI may take some time to translate text. When we call OpenAI from a script that uses tkinter to display a window, this delay can cause problems with our user interface. To eliminate these problems, we'll create a second thread in our script that asks OpenAI the question, while our program's main thread continues to manage our user interface. To create the second thread, we'll use Python's threading package (which we import) and we'll create a second thread to call our GetTranslation function which interacts with OpenAI:

```
import threading

def call_api_in_thread():
    # Function to call the API in a separate thread
    thread = threading.Thread(target=GetTranslation)
    thread.start()
```

Finally, the rest of our code creates our two text boxes and the Translate Text button. Don't worry too much yet about the code that builds the user interface. We'll see other programs that do similar processing and we'll discuss each, a little bit at a time.

When the user clicks the Translate Text button, the code will call our function call_api_in_thread which, in turn, calls OpenAI:

```
get_translation_button = tk.Button(root, text="Translate Text",
command=call_api_in_thread)
get_translation_button.pack()
```

Summary

In this chapter, you learned to use AI to translate text into a variety of languages. Your first program was pretty simple, but each time you wanted to translate different text or use a different language, you had to edit and save the program. Your second program was better in that it used the input function to ask the user for the text and the language. Finally, in the third program, you created a fancy user interface for the script.

In the next chapter, you will learn to use AI to create a simple chat bot with which you can interact.

Chapter 6
Coding an AI Chatbot

Chatbots are all around us. Companies of all types have chatbots on their Web pages that interact with customers. Many of these chatbots are driven by artificial intelligence. In this chapter, you will use the OpenAI API to create your own chatbot. However, unlike most chatbots that simply respond to a question with text, you are going to create a chatbot with attitude! In addition to asking your chatbot questions, you can tell your chatbot how you want it to respond:

- Normal chatbot
- A tired, cranky old lady
- An angry customer
- A circus announcer
- A horse-race announcer
- A newscaster
- And more

Let's look at some examples:

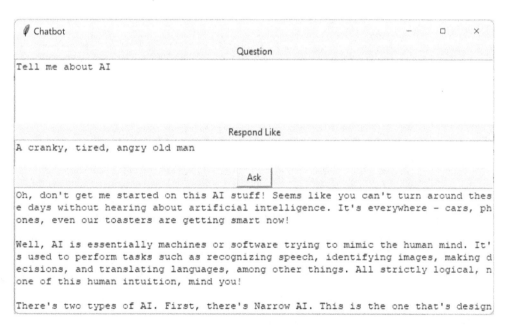

```
Chatbot                                              —   □   ×
                              Question
Tell me about California



                            Respond Like
A pirate|

                                Ask
Arr matey, let me tell ye 'bout this golden land known as California. Situated o
n the west coast of the United States, it's the richest and most populous state
in the union, so populous that if it were a country, it'd be the 5th largest eco
nomy in the world by GDP!

The terrain in California is as varied as the seafarers on a galleon. To the eas
t lie the great Sierra Nevada mountains, home to the gargantuan Lake Tahoe, the
largest alpine lake in North America, and Yosemite Valley, one of the grandest a
nd most splendid sights in all the seven seas!
```

```
Chatbot                                              —   □   ×
                              Question
Tell me about Microsoft



                            Respond Like
A very angry customer |

                                Ask
Geez, talk about Microsoft? Well alright, I don't exactly have a glowing review
for you, let me tell you.

So, Microsoft, that tech behemoth, was founded by Bill Gates and Paul Allen, bac
k in 1975. They started things off by creating a BASIC interpreter for the Micro
 Instrumentation and Telemetry Systems' (MITS) Altair 8800, a microcomputer. Yea
h, yeah, impressive, I guess.

But everyone knows them for their Windows operating system which apparently "rev
olutionized" personal computing. Pshh, how intuitive can an interface be if I ca
```

Understanding ChatGPT History and Context

When you interact with the ChatGPT prompt, ChatGPT remembers your
interactions to help it better put your conversation into context. Consider the
following example:

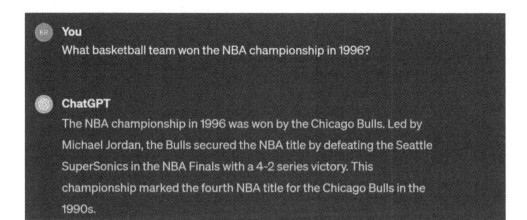

Next, I asked ChatGPT "Who was their coach?" The word "their" could mean any team, but because ChatGPT remembers our previous conversation, it gets the question right:

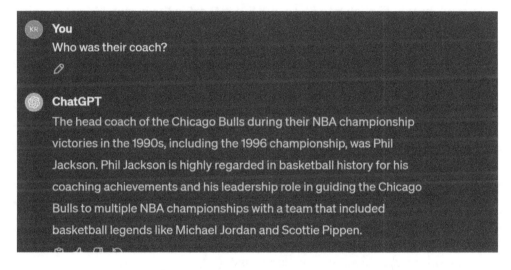

When you write a program that interacts with the OpenAPI ChatGPT API, you can pass the API history data that provides context similar to this. To run the ChatBot, you will use the following Python command:

C:\AIKids> python ChatBot.py <Enter>

The following code implements ChatBot.py. Again, you can run this program within the Jupyter AIKids Notebook you can download from my Web site at **http://www.class-files.com/ChatBot.html**:

import tkinter as tk

```python
from tkinter import filedialog
from openai import OpenAI
import os

key = os.getenv('OpenAI_API_Key')

# Set your OpenAI API key here
client = OpenAI(api_key = key)

messages = []
previous_respond_like = ""

# Function to handle the user's query
def handle_query():
  global messages, previous_respond_like

  send_button.config(state=tk.DISABLED)  # Disable the button
  # Get the user's query
  user_query = user_input.get(1.0, tk.END)
  message = {"role": "user", "content": user_query }
  messages.append(message)

  respond_like = "respond like " + respond_input.get(1.0, tk.END)
  message = {"role": "assistant", "content": respond_like }

  if message != previous_respond_like:
    messages.append(message)
    previous_respond_like = message

  # Call the ChatGPT model
  response = client.chat.completions.create(
    model="gpt-4",
    messages=messages
  )

  message = {"role": "system", "content":
response.choices[0].message.content}
  messages.append(message)

  bot_response.config(state=tk.NORMAL)
  bot_response.delete(1.0, tk.END)
  bot_response.insert(tk.END, response.choices[0].message.content)
```

```
    bot_response.config(state=tk.DISABLED)
    send_button.config(state=tk.NORMAL)  # Enable the button

import threading

def call_api_in_thread():
    # Function to call the API in a separate thread
    thread = threading.Thread(target=handle_query)
    thread.start()

# Create the main window
root = tk.Tk()
root.title("Chatbot")

question_label = tk.Label(root, text="Question")
question_label.pack()

user_input = tk.Text(root, height=5, width=80)
user_input.pack()

respond_like_label = tk.Label(root, text="Respond Like")
respond_like_label.pack()

respond_input = tk.Text(root, height=2, width=80)
respond_input.pack()

send_button = tk.Button(root, text="  Ask  ", command=call_api_in_thread)
send_button.pack()

bot_response = tk.Text(root, height=10, width=80)
bot_response.config(state=tk.DISABLED)
bot_response.pack()

# Start the main loop
root.mainloop()
```

Let's understand the code. The first few lines import the needed Python packages and provide your OpenAI API key to OpenAI:

```
import tkinter as tk
from tkinter import filedialog
from openai import OpenAI
```

```
import os

key = os.getenv('OpenAI_API_Key')

# Set your OpenAI API key here
client = OpenAI(api_key = key)
```

After the user types their question, optionally specifies how the chatbot should respond and clicks the Ask button, the code calls the handle_query function which does much of the work.

As discussed, the ChatBot remembers your previous interactions which provides message context to the ChatGPT API. Normally, when you pass a prompt to the API, you call the API specifying a user message similar to the following:

```
# Call the ChatGPT model
response = client.chat.completions.create(
  model="gpt-4",
  messages=[
   {"role": "user", "content": prompt_text}
  ]
)
```

To provide a historical context, you can send several messages include the user question and system reponses as shown here:

```
# Call the ChatGPT model
response = client.chat.completions.create(
  model="gpt-4",
  messages=[
   {"role": "user", "content": "Who was the star of the Chicago Bulls?"},
   {"role": "system", "content": "Michael Jordan was the Bulls Star",
   {"role": "user", "content": "When did he win his last championship?"},
   {"role": "system", "content": "1996"},
   {"role": "user", "content": "Did he play baseball?"},
  ]
)
```

To keep track of your questions and the system responses, the function uses a global variable called messages to which it appends each message. The function then passes that array of message to the OpenAI API each time it calls it:

```
# Call the ChatGPT model
response = client.chat.completions.create(
  model="gpt-4",
  messages=messages
)
```

In addition to user and system messages, the OpenAI ChatGPT API supports assistant messages which you can use to provide additional information. In this case, the function uses the assistant messages to tell the API how you want it to respond, such as a pirate or newscaster.

After the OpenAI ChatGPT API returns its result, the function displays the result in the output text box.

As discussed, OpenAI may take some time to create the image and generate the recipe. When we call OpenAI from a script that uses tkinter to display a window, this delay can cause problems with our user interface. To eliminate these problems, we'll create a second thread in our script that asks OpenAI the question, while our program's main thread continues to manage our user interface. To create the second thread, we'll use Python's threading package (which we import) and we'll create a second thread to call our handle_query function which interacts with OpenAI:

```
import threading
```

```
def call_api_in_thread():
    # Function to call the API in a separate thread
    thread = threading.Thread(target=handle_query)
    thread.start()
```

Finally, the rest of our code creates our text boxes and button.

Summary

In this chapter, you used OpenAI to create a custom chatbot. In the next chapter, you will learn to use the OpenAI API to generate your own images from a given text description of the message you desire! So, hold on, things are going to get fun!

Chapter
Generating Images Using AI

Just as you can use OpenAI and ChatGPT to generate text, you can also use OpenAI and the Dall-E model to create images. If you have used Microsoft Bing Image Creator, you have done just that.

Here's a few examples:

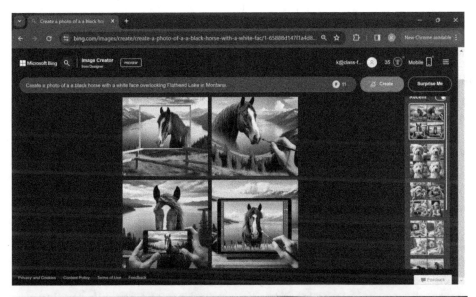

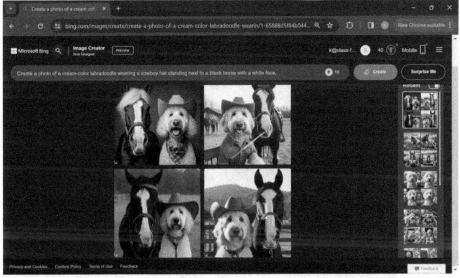

In this chapter, you will learn how to use AI to generate images within your own programs.

Creating a Quick Image with Your Own Program

Again, you can run this program using the AIKids Jupyter Notebook. If, instead, you are working from the Anaconda prompt, to create a simple application for creating images, start Notepad and type the following program. Remember, you can also download the program from my Web site and save the file as SimpleImage.py using your editor.

http://www.class-files.com/SimpleImage.html

The following code implements SimpleImage.py:

```
import io
import os
from openai import OpenAI

key = os.getenv('OpenAI_API_Key')

# Set your OpenAI API key here
client = OpenAI(api_key = key)

# Call the ChatGPT model
response = client.images.generate(
  model="dall-e-3",
  prompt="A cream-colored labradoodle in a library sleeping while reading a book.",
  size="1024x1024",
  quality="standard",
  n=1,)


print(response.data[0].url)
```

When you run the program, Python will display URL for the image that it creates as shown here:

C:\AIKids> python SimpleImage.py <Enter>
https://oaidalleapiprodscus.blob.core.windows.net/private/org-y1RQcjYjkbClltcrhbjTi2sb/user-HJGGXu7JCE3rLttIw8DdLmkG/img-Q0jqAZwyoHm9h5pfP3e7p7so.png?st=2023-12-24T15%3A19%3A25Z&se=2023-12-24T17%3A19%3A25Z&sp=r&sv=2021-08-

06&sr=b&rscd=inline&rsct=image/png&skoid=6aaadede-4fb3-4698-a8f6-684d7786b067&sktid=a48cca56-e6da-484e-a814-9c849652bcb3&skt=2023-12-23T23%3A25%3A29Z&ske=2023-12-24T23%3A25%3A29Z&sks=b&skv=2021-08-06&sig=Cj6Fw5roKbSGGkRLA5KFXS9YFhsgPzWEgQfpieLQlYk%3D

To display the image, Ctrl-Click on the URL or copy and paste the URL into your Web browser. You will see an image similar to that in Figure 7.1.

Figure 7.1: Using the OpenAI API to create an image.

To generate and display a different photo edit the script and change the line that uses the prompt parameter to describe your own image:

prompt="A cream-colored labradoodle in a library sleeping while reading a book.",

Save your program and run it again. This time, Python will display a link to your new image.

The code is very similar to the programs you created in previous chapters. The first three lines import the Python packages the code will use for OpenAI and to get your API key from the operating system. The next line gets your API key from the operating system so you don't hard code your key into your code where other people could see it. The next few lines set up OpenAI and then call the OpenAI API to generate the image. After OpenAI is done, the script displays the image URL.

Getting the Image Description from the User

The previous program worked—it generated our image. But each time you want to generate a different image, you had to change the program. A better program would ask the user for filename and then create the variatoins. To ask the user for the text and language, we can use the following statement:

description = input("Describe the image you want to create: ")

In this case, the input function will display a prompt on the screen for the user to enter the description of the image they desire. It will then assign whatever the user types to the variable description.

Using your text editor, create the following Python script, AskImage.py, which asks the user for their image description. Again, you can download this program from my Web site at **http://www.class-files.com/AskImage.html**.

```
import io
import os
from openai import OpenAI

key = os.getenv('OpenAI_API_Key')

# Set your OpenAI API key here
client = OpenAI(api_key = key)

description = input("Describe the image you want to create: ")

# Call the ChatGPT model
response = client.images.generate(
  model="dall-e-3",
  prompt=description,
  size="1024x1024",
  quality="standard",
  n=1,)

print(response.data[0].url)
```

When you run the script, Python will display the following output:

C:\AIKids> python AskImage.py <Enter>
Describe the image you want to create:

After you type your filename and press Enter, the script will generate your image variations.

Creating a Fancy Image-Generation Program

The previous two image-generation programs created images. The second program, AskImage.py, improved on the first by using the input function to get the image description from the user. The following Python script, Image.py, creates a fancier user interface, similar to that shown in Figure 7.2.

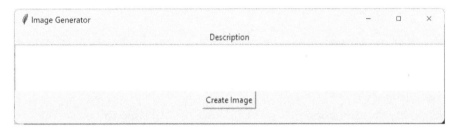

Figure 7.2: Prompting the user for description for the image they want to create.

After the user describes the image and clicks the Create Image button, the script will display the image as shown in Figure 7.3.

Figure 7.3 Generating and displaying an image.

The following code implements the Image.py script. You can download the program from my Web site at **http://www.class-files.com/Image.html**.

```python
import tkinter as tk
from PIL import Image, ImageTk
from openai import OpenAI
import os
import requests

api_key = os.getenv('OpenAI_API_Key')

# Set your OpenAI API key here
client = OpenAI(api_key = api_key)

def create_image():
    create_image_button.config(state=tk.DISABLED)  # Disable the button
    description = text_box.get('1.0', 'end-1c')

    # Call the ChatGPT model
    response = client.images.generate(
      model="dall-e-3",
      prompt=description,
      size="1024x1024",
      quality="standard",
      n=1,)

    image_response = requests.get(response.data[0].url)
    if image_response.status_code == 200:
      with open("image.png", 'wb') as f:
        f.write(image_response.content)
        f.close()

    image_path = "image.png"  # Path to the new image file
    image = Image.open(image_path)
    image.thumbnail((512, 512))  # Resize the image
    photo = ImageTk.PhotoImage(image)

    # Display the image in a label widget
    image_label.configure(image=photo)
    image_label.image = photo
    create_image_button.config(state=tk.NORMAL)  # Enable the button

import threading
```

```
def call_api_in_thread():
    # Function to call the API in a separate thread
    thread = threading.Thread(target=create_image)
    thread.start()

root = tk.Tk()
root.title("Image Generator")

# Description label and text box
label_description = tk.Label(root, text="Description")
label_description.pack()

text_box = tk.Text(root, height=4)
text_box.pack()

# Create Image button
create_image_button = tk.Button(root, text="Create Image",
command=call_api_in_thread)
create_image_button.pack()

# Image label to display the loaded image
image_label = tk.Label(root)
image_label.pack()

root.mainloop()
```

To run the script, use:

C:\AIKids> python Image.py <Enter>

Python will display the window previously shown in Figure 7.2, which you can use to describe your image.

Let's understand the code. Much of the code is similar to the first two programs you created in that it prompts ChatGPT to create images. The rest of the code builds the user interface that appears in the window.

The first few lines of the code tell Python which packages our program will use:

```
import tkinter as tk
from PIL import Image, ImageTk
from openai import OpenAI
import os
```

import requests

Next, the program gets your API key which it will use to call the OpenAI API and uses the key to prepare OpenAI for use:

```
key = os.getenv('OpenAI_API_Key')

# Set your OpenAI API key here
client = OpenAI(api_key = key)
```

The create_image function does most of the work:

```
def create_image():
  create_image_button.config(state=tk.DISABLED)  # Disable the button
  description = text_box.get('1.0', 'end-1c')

  # Call the ChatGPT model
  response = client.images.generate(
    model="dall-e-3",
    prompt=description,
    size="1024x1024",
    quality="standard",
    n=1,)

  image_response = requests.get(response.data[0].url)
  if image_response.status_code == 200:
    with open("image.png", 'wb') as f:
      f.write(image_response.content)
      f.close()

  image_path = "image.png"  # Path to the new image file
  image = Image.open(image_path)
  image.thumbnail((512, 512))  # Resize the image
  photo = ImageTk.PhotoImage(image)

  # Display the image in a label widget
  image_label.configure(image=photo)
  image_label.image = photo
  create_image_button.config(state=tk.NORMAL)  # Enable the button
```

To start, the program disables the Create Image button. That's because OpenAI may take some time to generate the image, so we disable the button the user can't click it again while OpenAI is working.

Next, the function gets the image_path and sends it to the OpenAI API asking for a 1024x1024 image based on the text description the user input. When the API completes, the function retrieves and saves the image on your disk as image.png.

The function then displays the image and re-enables the Create Image button.

As discussed, OpenAI may take some time to generate the variations. When we call OpenAI from a script that uses tkinter to display a window, this delay can cause problems with our user interface. To eliminate these problems, we'll create a second thread in our script that asks OpenAI to create the variations, while our program's main thread continues to manage our user interface. To create the second thread, we'll use Python's threading package (which we import) and we'll create a second thread to call our create_image function which interacts with OpenAI:

import threading

```
def call_api_in_thread():
    # Function to call the API in a separate thread
    thread = threading.Thread(target=create_image)
    thread.start()
```

Finally, the rest of our code creates the original user interface that lets the user describe the image they desire. When the user clicks the Create Image button, the code will call our function call_api_in_thread which, in turn, calls OpenAI:

```
# Create and place the button to get the joke
create_image_button = tk.Button(root, text="Create Image",
command=call_api_in_thread)
create_image_button.pack()
```

Summary

In this chapter, you learned to use AI to create images. Your first program was pretty simple, but each time you wanted to create a different image, you had to edit and save the program. Your second program was better in that it used the input function to ask the user for the image description. Finally, in the third program, you created a fancy user interface for the script.

In the next chapter, you will learn to use OpenAI to create variations of an image.

Chapter 8
Creating AI Variations of an Image

If you have used Microsoft Bing Image Creator to create images, you know that Image Creator will give you several variations of your image from which you can choose.

Here's a few examples:

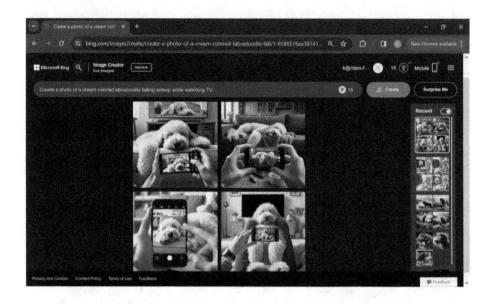

In this chapter, you will learn how to use AI to create variations of an existing image.

Creating Quick Variations of an Image

To create a simple application for creating image variations, start Notepad and type the following program. Remember, you can also download the program from my Web site and save the file as SimpleVariation.py using your editor.

http://www.class-files.com/SimpleVariation.html

The following code implements SimpleVariation.py:

```
import io
import os
from openai import OpenAI

key = os.getenv('OpenAI_API_Key')

# Set your OpenAI API key here
client = OpenAI(api_key = key)

response = client.images.create_variation(
  image=open("baxter.png", "rb"),
  n=4,
  size="512x512"
```

)

```
for i in range(4):
  print(response.data[i].url)
```

To run the program, I had the image file Baxter.png, shown in Figure 8.1, in my current folder.

Figure 8.1: The contents of the image file Baxter.png.

When you run the program, Python will display URLs for 4 images that it creates as shown here:

C:\AIKids> python SimpleVariation.py <Enter>
https://oaidalleapiprodscus.blob.core.windows.net/private/org-
y1RQcjYjkbClltcrhbjTi2sb/user-HJGGXu7JCE3rLttIw8DdLmkG/img-
Q0jqAZwyoHm9h5pfP3e7p7so.png?st=2023-12-
24T15%3A19%3A25Z&se=2023-12-24T17%3A19%3A25Z&sp=r&sv=2021-08-
06&sr=b&rscd=inline&rsct=image/png&skoid=6aaadede-4fb3-4698-a8f6-
684d7786b067&sktid=a48cca56-e6da-484e-a814-9c849652bcb3&skt=2023-12-
23T23%3A25%3A29Z&ske=2023-12-24T23%3A25%3A29Z&sks=b&skv=2021-
08-06&sig=Cj6Fw5roKbSGGkRLA5KFXS9YFhsgPzWEgQfpieLQlYk%3D
  ∷
https://oaidalleapiprodscus.blob.core.windows.net/private/org-
y1RQcjYjkbClltcrhbjTi2sb/user-HJGGXu7JCE3rLttIw8DdLmkG/img-
AnSKKVnxtEk1X5vejThw0Zg8.png?st=2023-12-24T15%3A19%3A24Z&se=2023-

12-24T17%3A19%3A24Z&sp=r&sv=2021-08-
06&sr=b&rscd=inline&rsct=image/png&skoid=6aaadede-4fb3-4698-a8f6-
684d7786b067&sktid=a48cca56-e6da-484e-a814-9c849652bcb3&skt=2023-12-
23T23%3A25%3A29Z&ske=2023-12-24T23%3A25%3A29Z&sks=b&skv=2021-
08-06&sig=SW/Y5TQGt9TSHs0uygi3acdPz0kjDJOFKj2rs9vI9WA%3D

To view the images, you can Ctrl+Click on the link or copy and paste the link into your browser. Your browser will display the images as shown in Figure 8.2.

Figure 8.2: Displaying image variations.

The following code implements SimpleVariation.py:

```
import io
import os
from openai import OpenAI
```

```
key = os.getenv('OpenAI_API_Key')

# Set your OpenAI API key here
client = OpenAI(api_key = key)

response = client.images.create_variation(
  image=open("baxter.png", "rb"),
  n=4,
  size="512x512"
)

for i in range(4):
  print(response.data[i].url)
```

To display variations of your own photo, edit the script and change the line that uses the image variable to specify your own filename:

```
  image=open("baxter.png", "rb"),
```

Save your program and run it again. This time, Python will display links to your image variations.

The code is very similar to the programs you created in previous chapters. The first three lines import the Python packages the code will use for OpenAI and to get your API key from the operating system. The next line gets your API key from the operating system so you don't hard code your key into your code where other people could see it. The next few lines set up OpenAI and then call the OpenAI API to get the translation. After OpenAI is done, the script uses a for loop to display the four image-variation links.

Getting the Input File from the User

The previous program worked—it created our image variations. But each time you want to use a different image, you have to change the program. A better program would ask the user for filename and then create the variations. To ask the user for the text and language, we can use the following statement:

image_file = input("What image file do you want to use? ")

In this case, the input function will display a prompt on the screen for the user to enter the file they desire. It will then assign whatever the user types to the variable image.

Using your text editor, create the following Python script, AskVariation.py, which asks the user for the input filename. You can download the program from my Web site at **http://www.class-files.com/AskVariation.html**.

```
import io
import os
from openai import OpenAI

key = os.getenv('OpenAI_API_Key')

# Set your OpenAI API key here
client = OpenAI(api_key = key)

image_file = input("What image file do you want to use? ")

response = client.images.create_variation(
    image=open(image_file, "rb"),
    n=4,
    size="512x512"
)

for i in range(4):
    print(response.data[i].url)
```

When you run the script, Python will display the following output:

```
C:\AIKids> python AskVariation.py  <Enter>
What image file do you want to use?
```

After you type your filename and press Enter, the script will generate your image variations.

Creating a Fancy Image-Variation Program

The previous two image-variation programs created variations of a image. The second program, AskVariation.py, improved on the first by using the input function to get the filename from the user. The following Python script, Variation.py, creates a fancier user interface, similar to that shown in Figure 8.3.

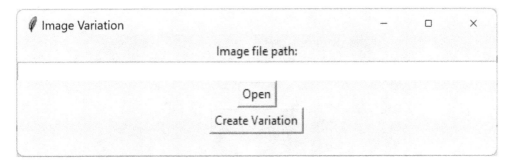

Figure 8.3: Prompting the user for image file for variations.

After the user selects a file, the script will display the original file's contents, as shown in Figure 8.4.

Figure 8.4: Displaying the file for variations.

After the user clicks the Create Variation button, the script will call ChatGPT to get the translation displaying the variations, as shown in Figure 8.5.

Figure 8.5 Displaying image variations.

The following code implements the Variation.py script which you can download from my Web site at **http://www.class-files.com/Variation.html**:

```
import tkinter as tk
from tkinter import filedialog
from openai import OpenAI
import base64
import os
import requests
from PIL import Image, ImageTk

api_key = os.getenv('OpenAI_API_Key')

# Set your OpenAI API key here
client = OpenAI(api_key = api_key)

def open_file():
    filepath = filedialog.askopenfilename(filetypes=[("Image files",
"*.jpg;*.png;*.jpeg")])
    if filepath:
        image_entry.delete(0, tk.END)
```

```
        image_entry.insert(0, filepath)

        img = Image.open(filepath)
        img = img.resize((256, 256))  # Resize image to 256x256
        photo = ImageTk.PhotoImage(img)

        # Display the image
        img_label.configure(image=photo)
        img_label.image = photo
        img_label.pack()

def GetVariations():
    global response
    variation_button.config(state=tk.DISABLED)  # Disable the button
    image_path = image_entry.get()

    if image_path:
        response = client.images.create_variation(
          image=open(image_path, "rb"),
          n=4,
          size="512x512"
        )

        for i in range(4):
          image_response = requests.get(response.data[i].url)
          if image_response.status_code == 200:
            with open(str(i)+".jpg", 'wb') as f:
              f.write(image_response.content)
              f.close()

        # Forget the original user interface
        image_label.pack_forget()
        image_entry.pack_forget()
        open_button.pack_forget()
        variation_button.pack_forget()
        img_label.pack_forget()

        # Create the 2x2 grid interface
        img_label01 = tk.Label(root)
        img_label01.grid(row=0, column=0, padx=10, pady=10)

        img_label02 = tk.Label(root)
```

```
img_label02.grid(row=0, column=1, padx=10, pady=10)

img_label03 = tk.Label(root)
img_label03.grid(row=1, column=0, padx=10, pady=10)

img_label04 = tk.Label(root)
img_label04.grid(row=1, column=1, padx=10, pady=10)

# display the image
img = Image.open("0.jpg")
img = img.resize((256, 256))  # Resize image to 256x256
photo = ImageTk.PhotoImage(img)

# Display the image
img_label01.configure(image=photo)
img_label01.image = photo

img = Image.open("1.jpg")
img = img.resize((256, 256))  # Resize image to 256x256
photo = ImageTk.PhotoImage(img)

# Display the image
img_label02.configure(image=photo)
img_label02.image = photo

img = Image.open("2.jpg")
img = img.resize((256, 256))  # Resize image to 256x256
photo = ImageTk.PhotoImage(img)

# Display the image
img_label03.configure(image=photo)
img_label03.image = photo

img = Image.open("3.jpg")
img = img.resize((256, 256))  # Resize image to 256x256
photo = ImageTk.PhotoImage(img)

# Display the image
img_label04.configure(image=photo)
img_label04.image = photo

else:
```

```
        result_text.delete(1.0, tk.END)
        result_text.insert(tk.END, "Please select an image.")

    variation_button.config(state=tk.NORMAL)  # Enable the button

import threading

def call_api_in_thread():
    # Function to call the API in a separate thread
    thread = threading.Thread(target=GetVariations)
    thread.start()

# Create the main window
root = tk.Tk()
root.title("Image Variation")

# Create text entry for image path
image_label = tk.Label(root, text="Image file path:")
image_label.pack()
image_entry = tk.Entry(root, width=80)
image_entry.pack()

# Create button to open file
open_button = tk.Button(root, text="Open", command=open_file)
open_button.pack()

# Create button to get variations
variation_button = tk.Button(root, text="Create Variation",
command=call_api_in_thread)
variation_button.pack()

# Image display label
img_label = tk.Label(root)
img_label.pack()

# Start the GUI
root.mainloop()
```

To run the script, use:

C:\AIKids> python Variation.py <Enter>

Python will display the window previously shown in Figure 8.3, which you can use to select your image for variations.

Let's understand the code. Much of the code is similar to the first two programs you created in that it prompts ChatGPT to create variations. The rest of the code builds the user interface that appears in the window. The script actually uses two user-interfaces. The first displays the screen that prompts the user for and then displays the selected file. The second user interface creates the 2x2 grid within which it displays the image variations.

The first three lines of the code tell Python which packages our program will use:

```
import tkinter as tk
from tkinter import filedialog
from openai import OpenAI
import base64
import os
import requests
from PIL import Image, ImageTk
```

Next, the program gets your API key which it will use to call the OpenAI API and uses the key to prepare OpenAI for use:

```
key = os.getenv('OpenAI_API_Key')

# Set your OpenAI API key here
client = OpenAI(api_key = key)
```

The GetVariations function does most of the work:

```
def GetVariations():
  global response
  variation_button.config(state=tk.DISABLED)  # Disable the button
  image_path = image_entry.get()

  if image_path:
    response = client.images.create_variation(
      image=open(image_path, "rb"),
      n=4,
      size="512x512"
    )
```

```
for i in range(4):
  image_response = requests.get(response.data[i].url)
  if image_response.status_code == 200:
    with open(str(i)+".jpg", 'wb') as f:
      f.write(image_response.content)
      f.close()

# Forget the original user interface
image_label.pack_forget()
image_entry.pack_forget()
open_button.pack_forget()
variation_button.pack_forget()
img_label.pack_forget()

# Create the 2x2 grid interface
img_label01 = tk.Label(root)
img_label01.grid(row=0, column=0, padx=10, pady=10)

img_label02 = tk.Label(root)
img_label02.grid(row=0, column=1, padx=10, pady=10)

img_label03 = tk.Label(root)
img_label03.grid(row=1, column=0, padx=10, pady=10)

img_label04 = tk.Label(root)
img_label04.grid(row=1, column=1, padx=10, pady=10)

# display the image
img = Image.open("0.jpg")
img = img.resize((256, 256))  # Resize image to 256x256
photo = ImageTk.PhotoImage(img)

# Display the image
img_label01.configure(image=photo)
img_label01.image = photo

img = Image.open("1.jpg")
img = img.resize((256, 256))  # Resize image to 256x256
photo = ImageTk.PhotoImage(img)

# Display the image
img_label02.configure(image=photo)
```

```
        img_label02.image = photo

        img = Image.open("2.jpg")
        img = img.resize((256, 256))  # Resize image to 256x256
        photo = ImageTk.PhotoImage(img)

        # Display the image
        img_label03.configure(image=photo)
        img_label03.image = photo

        img = Image.open("3.jpg")
        img = img.resize((256, 256))  # Resize image to 256x256
        photo = ImageTk.PhotoImage(img)

        # Display the image
        img_label04.configure(image=photo)
        img_label04.image = photo

    else:
        result_text.delete(1.0, tk.END)
        result_text.insert(tk.END, "Please select an image.")

    variation_button.config(state=tk.NORMAL)  # Enable the button
```

To start, the program disables the Get Variation button. That's because OpenAI may take some time to perform the translation, so we disable the button the user can't click it again while OpenAI is working.

Next, the function gets the image_path and sends it to the OpenAI API asking for four 512x512 image variations. When the API completes, the function uses a for loop to save the four variations in the files 0.jpg, 1.jpg, 2.jpg, and 3.jpg.

The code then "forgets" the original user-interface and creates a 2x2 grid to hold the images. The function then opens each image one image at a time, resizing the image to 256x256 and displaying it in the corresponding location.

As discussed, OpenAI may take some time to generate the variations. When we call OpenAI from a script that uses tkinter to display a window, this delay can cause problems with our user interface. To eliminate these problems, we'll create a second thread in our script that asks OpenAI to create the variations, while our program's main thread continues to manage our user interface. To create the second thread, we'll use Python's threading package (which we import) and we'll create a second thread to call our GetVariations function which interacts with OpenAI:

import threading

```
def call_api_in_thread():
    # Function to call the API in a separate thread
    thread = threading.Thread(target=GetVariations)
    thread.start()
```

Finally, the rest of our code creates the original user interface that lets the user select and display a photo image.

When the user clicks the Get Variation button, the code will call our function call_api_in_thread which, in turn, calls OpenAI:

```
# Create and place the button to get the joke
variation_button = tk.Button(root, text="Get Variation",
command=call_api_in_thread)
variation_button.pack()
```

Summary

In this chapter, you learned to use AI to create variations of an image. Your first program was pretty simple, but each time you wanted to use a different image, you had to edit and save the program. Your second program was better in that it used the input function to ask the user for the image file. Finally, in the third program, you created a fancy user interface for the script.

In the next chapter, you will learn to use AI to perform computer vision, which directs AI to describe the contents of a photo.

Chapter 9
Coding Computer Vision

Computer vision describes the ability of AI to view and understand the contents within a photo. When your phone recognizes you, it is performing computer vision. When a security camera monitors passengers at an airport, it uses computer vision. Here's a few examples:

Photo:

Computer Vision:

This is an image of two children in a high-tech environment, seemingly engaged in some form of digital interaction or study. The young girl is focused on the monitor in front of her, on which there is a 3D wireframe animation or rendering of a dog's head. She is pointing at the screen and might be learning about the structure of the dog or engaging in a computer-aided design activity. The boy, standing beside her, is attentively looking at the same screen. They both wear casual hoodies and the color scheme of the room suggests a futuristic or advanced technological setting, with neon blue lights and multiple screens showing various data or graphics related to the dog's head. Their interaction with technology gives the impression that they might be learning about animals, biology, or participating in a computer science-related activity. The complexity and sophistication of the environment suggest that they are in a specialized setting, possibly an educational facility equipped with advanced technological resources.

Photo:

Computer Vision:

This is a charming photo showing a man sitting on a couch with a laptop, seemingly absorbed in his work. Interestingly, a medium-sized brown dog is sitting next to him in a very human-like posture, with the laptop between its paws, as if the dog is mirroring the man's behavior or pretending to work on the computer as well. The room has a cozy feel with soft lighting and visible decor elements that suggest a homey atmosphere. The dog's attention towards the camera, with its head slightly tilted, adds a comical and endearing touch to the scene.

In this chapter, you will create programs that perform computer vision.

Creating a Quick Computer-Vision Program

To create a simple computer-vision application, start Notepad and type the following program. Remember, you can also download the program from my Web site and save the file as SimpleVision.py using your editor.

http://www.class-files.com/SimpleVision.html

To run the program, you will need to have a file with a photo in your current folder. The file should be a .png or .jpg file. In my case, I have the file Robot.jpg which contains the image shown in Figure 9.1.

Figure 9.1: The robot in the file *robot.png*.

The following code implements SimpleVision.py:

When I run the program, Python will display the following output:

C:\AIKids> python SimpleVision.py <Enter>
{"message": "The image depicts a highly detailed, realistic-looking humanoid robot seated on a sleek, modern chair. The robot has a silver metallic body with intricate mechanical details, such as joints and gears, visible throughout its design. Its head includes two glowing blue eyes and it appears to be gazing thoughtfully or attentively to its left. The setting is a futuristic interior, possibly a command center or a lab, characterized by ambient blue lighting, reflective surfaces, and advanced computer interfaces with holographic displays showing data and digital figures.

The environment conveys a clean and high-tech atmosphere, with an expansive room that includes more chairs and workstations in the background,

as well as large transparent screens displaying various types of information. The robot's design suggests advanced technology, possibly indicating that it could be capable of performing complex tasks or maybe even possessing artificial intelligence."}

The following Python code implements SimpleVision.py:

```python
from openai import OpenAI
import requests
import os
import base64

api_key = os.getenv('OpenAI_API_Key')

# Set your OpenAI API key here
client = OpenAI(api_key = api_key)

# Function to encode the image
def encode_image(image_path):
  with open(image_path, "rb") as image_file:
    return base64.b64encode(image_file.read()).decode('utf-8')

# Path to your image
image_path = 'Robot.png' # Replace with the name of your file

# Getting the base64 string
base64_image = encode_image(image_path)

headers = {
  "Content-Type": "application/json",
  "Authorization": f"Bearer {api_key}"
}

payload = {
  "model": "gpt-4-vision-preview",
  "messages": [
    {
      "role": "user",
      "content": [
        {
          "type": "text",
          "text": 'Describe the image'
        },
```

```
    {
      "type": "image_url",
      "image_url": {
        "url": f"data:image/jpeg;base64,{base64_image}"
      }
    }
   ]
  }
 ],
  "max_tokens": 300
}

response = requests.post("https://api.openai.com/v1/chat/completions",
headers=headers, json=payload)

data = response.json()  # Parse the JSON response

# Access specific data from the response
choices = data['choices']  # Access the 'choices' array
first_choice = choices[0]  # Access the first choice in the array

# Access content from the first choice
content = first_choice['message']['content']
content = content.replace('"', '"""')

print('{"message": "' + content + '"}')
```

To change your program so it describes a different image, edit the line the line
that contains the image_path variable and replace the name Robot.png with the
name of your image file:

image_path = 'Robot.png' # Replace with the name of your file

Save your program and run it again. This time, Python will display output
describing your image.

With respect to using AI, this code is very similar to the programs you created
throughout this book. It gets your API key, calls the OpenAI and then displays the
API's result. However, because it must pass an image to OpenAI, how this script
calls the API is a little different.

To pass the image photo to the OpenAI API, the script reads the file from your folder and puts the file in a specific format, called Base64, that it can use to pass the image to the OpenAI AI. To encode the photo into Base64, the script uses the following function that reads and encodes the image:

```
# Function to encode the image
def encode_image(image_path):
  with open(image_path, "rb") as image_file:
    return base64.b64encode(image_file.read()).decode('utf-8')
```

To encode your file using the function, the script uses the following statement:

```
# Getting the base64 string
base64_image = encode_image(image_path)
```

As discussed, because it is passing a photo the OpenAI, to call the OpenAI API, this script uses a technique that is different from what you have been using. The script packages up the image and other data it must send to the API in a format called JSON (which stands for JavaScript Object Notation). You can think of JSON as a format that lets us package up different kinds of information for exchanging the content with a different program—in this case, the OpenAI API. The following code packages the message into JSON format:

```
headers = {
  "Content-Type": "application/json",
  "Authorization": f"Bearer {api_key}"
}

payload = {
  "model": "gpt-4-vision-preview",
  "messages": [
    {
      "role": "user",
      "content": [
        {
          "type": "text",
          "text": 'Describe the image'
        },
        {
          "type": "image_url",
          "image_url": {
```

```
      "url": f"data:image/jpeg;base64,{base64_image}"
    }
   }
  ]
 }
],
 "max_tokens": 300
}
```

To call the OpenAI API, we specify the add API's URL, passing the data to it:

response = requests.post("https://api.openai.com/v1/chat/completions", headers=headers, json=payload)

When the API completes its analysis of the image, we unpack the JSON it returns to us and then display the result:

```
data = response.json()  # Parse the JSON response

# Access specific data from the response
choices = data['choices']  # Access the 'choices' array
first_choice = choices[0]  # Access the first choice in the array

# Access content from the first choice
content = first_choice['message']['content']
content = content.replace('"', '"""')

print('{"message": "' + content + '"}')
```

Getting the Image from the User

The previous program worked—it analyzed our photo. But each time we want to analyze a different photo, we must change the program. A better program would ask the user for photo they want to analyze. To ask the user for a image file, we can use the following statement:

image_path = input("What photo file do you want to analyze? ")

In this case, the input function will display a prompt on the screen for the user to enter a photo filename. It will then assign the filename the user types to the image_path.

Using your text editor, create the following Python script, AskVision.py, which asks the user for the image to analyze and then displays the computer-vision result. You can download the program from my Web site at **http://www.class-files.com/AskVision.html**.

```python
from openai import OpenAI
import requests
import os
import base64

api_key = os.getenv('OpenAI_API_Key')

# Set your OpenAI API key here
client = OpenAI(api_key = api_key)

# Function to encode the image
def encode_image(image_path):
  with open(image_path, "rb") as image_file:
    return base64.b64encode(image_file.read()).decode('utf-8')

# Path to your image
image_path = input("What photo file do you want to analyze? ")

# Getting the base64 string
base64_image = encode_image(image_path)

headers = {
  "Content-Type": "application/json",
  "Authorization": f"Bearer {api_key}"
}

payload = {
  "model": "gpt-4-vision-preview",
  "messages": [
    {
      "role": "user",
      "content": [
        {
          "type": "text",
          "text": 'Describe the image'
        },
        {
```

```
      "type": "image_url",
      "image_url": {
        "url": f"data:image/jpeg;base64,{base64_image}"
      }
    }
  ]
 }
],
"max_tokens": 300
}

response = requests.post("https://api.openai.com/v1/chat/completions",
headers=headers, json=payload)

data = response.json()  # Parse the JSON response

# Access specific data from the response
choices = data['choices']  # Access the 'choices' array
first_choice = choices[0]  # Access the first choice in the array

# Access content from the first choice
content = first_choice['message']['content']
content = content.replace("", "")

print('{"message": "' + content + '"}')
```

I ran the script with the file Image1.png which contains the three dogs shown in Figure 9.2.

Figure 9.2: The contents of my file Image1.png.

When I ran the program, I got the following output:

C:\AIKids> python AskImage.py
What photo file do you want to analyze? image1.png

{"message": "The image is a humorous and heavily stylized depiction of three dogs posed as if they are wealthy and powerful figures. The setting appears to be a luxurious wooden cabin with large windows that offer a view of a body of water and a forested coastline.

Center stage is a golden Labrador Retriever, sitting back with a cigar in its mouth, projecting an air of authority. To the left is a Golden Retriever, looking slightly up with a relaxed expression. On the right is a German Shepherd, seated upright and looking directly at the camera with an attentive gaze.

In front of these canine characters is a large, old-fashioned pot brimming with gold coins, suggesting an abundance of wealth. The overall composition of the image conveys a whimsical, anthropomorphic fantasy where dogs are depicted in human-like roles of opulence and power. The image is designed to be amusing and is likely intended to be a playful artwork rather than a representation of a real scenario."}

Creating a Fancy Computer-Vision Program

The previous two computer-vision programs analyzed photos. The second program, AskVision.py, improved on the first by using the input function to get the image file from the user. The following Python script, Vision.py, creates a fancier user interface, similar to that shown in Figure 9.3.

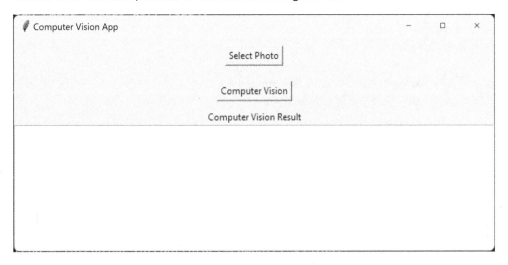

Figure 9.3: Prompting the user for a file to analyze.

The window contains a button the user can click to select their file. After the user does so and clicks the Computer Vision button, the script displays the result, as shown in Figure 9.4.

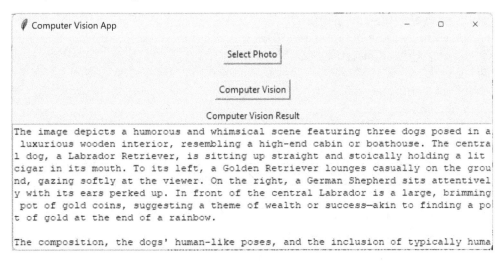

Figure 9.4: Displaying the computer-vision result within a text box.

The following code implements the Vision.py script. You can download the script from my Web site at **http://www.class-files.com/Vision.html**.

```python
import tkinter as tk
from tkinter import filedialog
from openai import OpenAI
import requests
import os
import base64

api_key = os.getenv('OpenAI_API_Key')
image_path = "" # the file to analyze

# Set your OpenAI API key here
client = OpenAI(api_key = api_key)

# Function to encode the image
def encode_image(image_path):
  with open(image_path, "rb") as image_file:
    return base64.b64encode(image_file.read()).decode('utf-8')

def select_photo():
    global image_path
    file_path = filedialog.askopenfilename(filetypes=[("Image Files",
"*.jpg;*.jpeg;*.png;*.gif")])
    if file_path:
        image_path = file_path
        entry_result.delete(1.0, tk.END)
        entry_result.insert(tk.END, file_path)

def get_computer_vision():
  global image_path
  if image_path != "":
    entry_result.delete(1.0, tk.END)
    button_computer_vision.config(state=tk.DISABLED)  # Disable the button
    button_select_photo.config(state=tk.DISABLED)  # Disable the

    # Getting the base64 string
    base64_image = encode_image(image_path)

    headers = {
      "Content-Type": "application/json",
      "Authorization": f"Bearer {api_key}"
```

```
    }

    payload = {
      "model": "gpt-4-vision-preview",
      "messages": [
        {
          "role": "user",
          "content": [
            {
              "type": "text",
              "text": 'Describe the image'
            },
            {
              "type": "image_url",
              "image_url": {
              "url": f"data:image/jpeg;base64,{base64_image}"
              }
            }
          ]
        }
      ],
        "max_tokens": 300
    }

    response = requests.post("https://api.openai.com/v1/chat/completions",
headers=headers, json=payload)

    data = response.json()  # Parse the JSON response

    # Access specific data from the response
    choices = data['choices']  # Access the 'choices' array
    first_choice = choices[0]  # Access the first choice in the array

    # Access content from the first choice
    content = first_choice['message']['content']
    content = content.replace('"', "'")

    entry_result.insert(tk.END, content)

    button_computer_vision.config(state=tk.NORMAL)  # Enable the button
    button_select_photo.config(state=tk.NORMAL)  # Enable the
  else:
```

```
    entry_result.delete(1.9, tk.END)
    entry_result.insert(tk.END, "You must select a file")

import threading

def call_api_in_thread():
    # Function to call the API in a separate thread
    thread = threading.Thread(target=get_computer_vision)
    thread.start()

root = tk.Tk()
root.title("Computer Vision App")

# Function buttons
button_select_photo = tk.Button(root, text="Select Photo",
command=select_photo)
button_select_photo.pack(pady=10)

button_computer_vision = tk.Button(root, text="Computer Vision",
command=call_api_in_thread)
button_computer_vision.pack(pady=10)

# Result text box
label_result = tk.Label(root, text="Computer Vision Result")
label_result.pack()

entry_result = tk.Text(root, width=80, height=10)
entry_result.pack()

root.mainloop()
```

Again, type the code using your text editor, or, download the code from my Web site at **http://www.class-files.com/Vision.html**.

To run the script, use:

C:\AIKids> python Vision.py <Enter>

Python will display the window previously shown in Figure 9.3, which you can use to ask the user for a file.

Let's understand the code. Much of the code is similar to the first two programs you created in that it prompts ChatGPT to return a joke. The rest of the code builds the user interface that appears in the window.

The first lines of the code tell Python which packages our program will use:

```
import tkinter as tk
from tkinter import filedialog
from openai import OpenAI
import requests
import os
import base64
```

Next, the program gets your API key which it will use to call the OpenAI API and uses the key to prepare OpenAI for use:

```
key = os.getenv('OpenAI_API_Key')

# Set your OpenAI API key here
client = OpenAI(api_key = key)
```

To send the image file to the OpenAI API, we must encode the photo into Base64 format. The function encode_image does that:

```
# Function to encode the image
def encode_image(image_path):
  with open(image_path, "rb") as image_file:
    return base64.b64encode(image_file.read()).decode('utf-8')
```

To let the user select the image file using an Open dialog box, we create the following function which assigns the path of the file the user selects to the variable image_path:

```
def select_photo():
  global image_path
  file_path = filedialog.askopenfilename(filetypes=[("Image Files",
"*.jpg;*.jpeg;*.png;*.gif")])
  if file_path:
    image_path = file_path
    entry_result.delete(1.0, tk.END)
    entry_result.insert(tk.END, file_path)
```

The get_computer_vision function does most of the work:

```python
def get_computer_vision():
 global image_path
 if image_path != "":
  button_computer_vision.config(state=tk.DISABLED)  # Disable the button
  button_select_photo.config(state=tk.DISABLED)  # Disable the
  entry_result.delete(1.0, tk.END)

  # Getting the base64 string
  base64_image = encode_image(image_path)

  headers = {
    "Content-Type": "application/json",
    "Authorization": f"Bearer {api_key}"
  }

  payload = {
    "model": "gpt-4-vision-preview",
    "messages": [
      {
        "role": "user",
        "content": [
         {
           "type": "text",
           "text": 'Describe the image'
         },
         {
           "type": "image_url",
           "image_url": {
             "url": f"data:image/jpeg;base64,{base64_image}"
           }
         }
        ]
      }
    ],
      "max_tokens": 300
  }

  response = requests.post("https://api.openai.com/v1/chat/completions",
headers=headers, json=payload)

  data = response.json()  # Parse the JSON response
```

```
    # Access specific data from the response
    choices = data['choices']  # Access the 'choices' array
    first_choice = choices[0]  # Access the first choice in the array

    # Access content from the first choice
    content = first_choice['message']['content']
    content = content.replace('"', '"""')

    entry_result.insert(tk.END, content)

    button_computer_vision.config(state=tk.NORMAL)  # Enable the button
    button_select_photo.config(state=tk.NORMAL)  # Enable the
  else:
    entry_result.delete(1.9, tk.END)
    entry_result.insert(tk.END, "You must select a file")
```

To start, the function uses an if statement to make sure the user has selected an image file. If the user has selected a file, the function disables the buttons. That's because OpenAI may take some time to analyze the image. As such, we disable the buttons the user can't click them again while OpenAI is working.

Next, the code deletes the results from the text box so it is empty for us to display the computer-vision result within.

Next, we encode the image and call OpenAI to get the computer-vision result. When OpenAI is done, we insert the text into the output text box and we re-enable the buttons so the user can analyze another image if they want.

As discussed, OpenAI may take some time to analyze the image. When we call OpenAI from a script that uses tkinter to display a window, this delay can cause problems with our user interface. To eliminate these problems, we'll create a second thread in our script that asks OpenAI the question, while our program's main thread continues to manage our user interface. To create the second thread, we'll use Python's threading package (which we import) and we'll create a second thread to call our get_computer_vision function which interacts with OpenAI:

```
import threading

def call_api_in_thread():
    # Function to call the API in a separate thread
```

```
thread = threading.Thread(target=get_computer_vision)
thread.start()
```

Finally, the rest of our code creates our text box and buttons.

Summary

In this chapter, you learned to use AI to perform computer vision. Your first program was pretty simple, but each time you wanted a different image, you had to edit and save the program. Your second program was better in that it used the input function to ask the user for the image file. Finally, in the third program, you created a fancy user interface for the script.

In the next chapter, you will learn to use OpenAI to create a simple recipe generator.

Chapter 10
Coding an AI Recipe Generator

Cooking is a lot like coding—you need to follow steps and perform the given instructions. In this chapter, you will leverage AI to produce a recipe for your desired meal. Your code will create an image of the desired meal, a list of the ingredients you will need, and your recipe. When the recipe is complete, you can click a button to produce a PDF with everything you need.

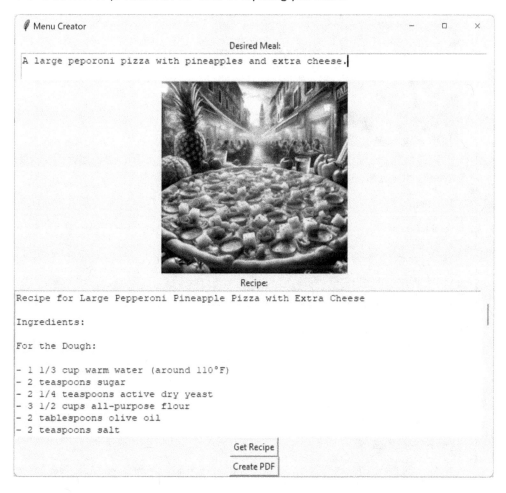

AI Recipe Generator

Recipe for Large Pepperoni Pineapple Pizza with Extra Cheese

Ingredients:

For the Dough:

- 1 1/3 cup warm water (around 110°F)
- 2 teaspoons sugar
- 2 1/4 teaspoons active dry yeast
- 3 1/2 cups all-purpose flour
- 2 tablespoons olive oil
- 2 teaspoons salt

For the Topping:

- 1 cup pizza sauce
- 3 cups shredded mozzarella cheese
- 2 cups sliced pepperoni
- 1 cup diced fresh pineapple
- 1 cup extra cheese (You can use extra mozzarella or mix with cheddar or Monterey Jack)

Preparation Steps:

1. Combine the warm water and sugar in a bowl and stir it until the sugar has dissolved. Sprinkle the yeast over the water and let it sit for 5 minutes until the mixture is foamy.

2. In a large bowl, combine the flour and salt, make a well in the center and add the yeast mixture

Ideally, you will run this program using the AIKids Jupyter Notebook. Before you can run this program, you need to install fpdf using pip:

C:\AIKids> pip install fpdf <Enter>

The following code implements Recipe.py. You can download the program from my Web site at **http://www.class-files.com/Recipe.html**.

```python
import tkinter as tk
from tkinter import scrolledtext
from PIL import Image, ImageTk
from fpdf import FPDF  # For creating PDF
from openai import OpenAI
import os
import requests

api_key = os.getenv('OpenAI_API_Key')

# Set your OpenAI API key here
client = OpenAI(api_key = api_key)

def create_image():
    description = "Create an image of a " + desired_meal_entry.get('1.0', 'end-1c')

    # Call the ChatGPT model
    response = client.images.generate(
      model="dall-e-3",
      prompt=description,
      size="1024x1024",
      quality="standard",
      n=1,)

    image_response = requests.get(response.data[0].url)
    if image_response.status_code == 200:
      with open("image.png", 'wb') as f:
        f.write(image_response.content)
        f.close()

    image_path = "image.png"  # Path to the new image file
    image = Image.open(image_path)
    image.thumbnail((256, 256))  # Resize the image
    photo = ImageTk.PhotoImage(image)
```

```python
    # Display the image in a label widget
    image_label.configure(image=photo)
    image_label.image = photo

def get_recipe():
  desired_meal = desired_meal_entry.get("1.0", "end-1c")
  if desired_meal:
    get_recipe_button.config(state=tk.DISABLED)  # Disable the button
    create_pdf_button.config(state=tk.DISABLED)  # Disable the button

    recipe_text.delete(1.0, tk.END)  # Clear any existing text
    recipe_text.insert(tk.END, "Processing...")

    create_image()

    description = "Get a recipe for a " + desired_meal

    # Call the ChatGPT model
    response = client.chat.completions.create(
      model="gpt-4",
      messages=[
      {"role": "user", "content": description}
      ]
      )
    recipe_text.delete(1.0, tk.END)  # Clear any existing text

    recipe_text.insert(tk.END, response.choices[0].message.content)
    get_recipe_button.config(state=tk.NORMAL)  # Enable the button
    create_pdf_button.config(state=tk.NORMAL)  # Enable the button
  else:
    recipe_text.delete(1.0, tk.END)  # Clear any existing text
    recipe_text.insert(tk.END, "Must specify a desired meal")

def create_pdf():
    recipe = recipe_text.get("1.0", "end-1c")

    pdf = FPDF()
    pdf.add_page()
    pdf.set_font("Arial", size=12)
    pdf.cell(200, 10, txt="AI Recipe Generator", ln=True)
    pdf.ln(10)
```

```
    # image = Image.open("image.jpg")
     pdf.image("image.png", x=10, y=pdf.get_y(), w=100)
     pdf.ln(110)
     pdf.multi_cell(0, 5, txt=recipe)

     pdf.output("Menu.pdf")

import threading

def call_api_in_thread():
    # Function to call the API in a separate thread
    thread = threading.Thread(target=get_recipe)
    thread.start()

root = tk.Tk()
root.title("Menu Creator")

# Desired Meal Label and Entry
desired_meal_label = tk.Label(root, text="Desired Meal:")
desired_meal_label.pack()

desired_meal_entry = tk.Text(root, height=2, width=80)
desired_meal_entry.pack()

image_label = tk.Label(root)
image_label.pack()

# Recipe Textbox with Scrollbar
recipe_label = tk.Label(root, text="Recipe:")
recipe_label.pack()

recipe_text = scrolledtext.ScrolledText(root, width=80, height=12,
wrap=tk.WORD)
recipe_text.pack()

# Get Recipe and Create PDF Buttons
get_recipe_button = tk.Button(root, text="Get Recipe",
command=call_api_in_thread)
get_recipe_button.pack()

create_pdf_button = tk.Button(root, text="Create PDF", command=create_pdf)
```

```
create_pdf_button.pack()

root.mainloop()
```

Let's understand the code. The first few lines import the needed Python packages and provide your OpenAI API key to OpenAI:

```
import tkinter as tk
from tkinter import scrolledtext
from PIL import Image, ImageTk
from fpdf import FPDF  # For creating PDF
from openai import OpenAI
import os
import requests

api_key = os.getenv('OpenAI_API_Key')

# Set your OpenAI API key here
client = OpenAI(api_key = api_key)
```

After the user types the meal they desire and clicks the Get Recipe button, the code calls the get_recipe function which does much of the work. The function uses an if statement to check that the user has specified the desired meal. If so, it then disables the buttons to prevent the user from clicking them while OpenAI is getting the image and recipe. The function then calls the create_image function which generates and displays an image appropriate for the meal.

Next, the function calls the OpenAI API to get the recipe. When the API completes, the function displays it within the text box and re-enables the buttons.

```
def get_recipe():
  desired_meal = desired_meal_entry.get("1.0", "end-1c")
  if desired_meal:
   get_recipe_button.config(state=tk.DISABLED)  # Disable the button
   create_pdf_button.config(state=tk.DISABLED)  # Disable the button

   recipe_text.delete(1.0, tk.END)  # Clear any existing text
   recipe_text.insert(tk.END, "Processing...")

   create_image()
```

```
    description = "Get a recipe for a " + desired_meal

    # Call the ChatGPT model
    response = client.chat.completions.create(
      model="gpt-4",
      messages=[
      {"role": "user", "content": description}
      ]
    )
    recipe_text.delete(1.0, tk.END)  # Clear any existing text

    recipe_text.insert(tk.END, response.choices[0].message.content)
    get_recipe_button.config(state=tk.NORMAL)  # Enable the button
    create_pdf_button.config(state=tk.NORMAL)  # Enable the button
  else:
    recipe_text.delete(1.0, tk.END)  # Clear any existing text
    recipe_text.insert(tk.END, "Must specify a desired meal")
```

The create_image function uses OpenAI to generate an appropriate picture for the meal and then saves the image in your folder with the name image.png. The code then displays the image.

As discussed, OpenAI may take some time to create the image and generate the recipe. When we call OpenAI from a script that uses tkinter to display a window, this delay can cause problems with our user interface. To eliminate these problems, we'll create a second thread in our script that asks OpenAI the question, while our program's main thread continues to manage our user interface. To create the second thread, we'll use Python's threading package (which we import) and we'll create a second thread to call our get_recipe function which interacts with OpenAI:

```
import threading

def call_api_in_thread():
    # Function to call the API in a separate thread
    thread = threading.Thread(target=get_recipe)
    thread.start()
```

To produce the PDF, the code uses the create_pdf function which leverages the Python FPDF package. The function creates a PDF, adds a page and then writes a title on the page. Next, the function displays the image followed by the recipe text:

```
def create_pdf():
    recipe = recipe_text.get("1.0", "end-1c")

    pdf = FPDF()
    pdf.add_page()
    pdf.set_font("Arial", size=12)
    pdf.cell(200, 10, txt="AI Recipe Generator", ln=True)
    pdf.ln(10)

    pdf.image("image.png", x=10, y=pdf.get_y(), w=100)
    pdf.ln(110)
    pdf.multi_cell(0, 5, txt=recipe)

    pdf.output("Menu.pdf")
```

Finally, the rest of our code creates our text box and buttons.

Summary

In this chapter, you used OpenAI to generate text and an image—producing your recipe generator. You also learned how to print content to a PDF. In the next chapter, you will perform similar processing to use AI to generate a card appropriate for birthdays and other holidays and events.

Chapter 11
Creating an AI-Driven Card Maker

Throughout this book, you have learned to create applications that use AI to generate text and images. In this chapter, you will create a CardMaker application that generates a card appropriate for events such as birthdays, graduations, and other holidays.

The application will create a PDF for which you can print the first page, turnover the paper and insert it back into the printer, and then print the second page. The end result will be a card you can fold in half, similar to that shown here.

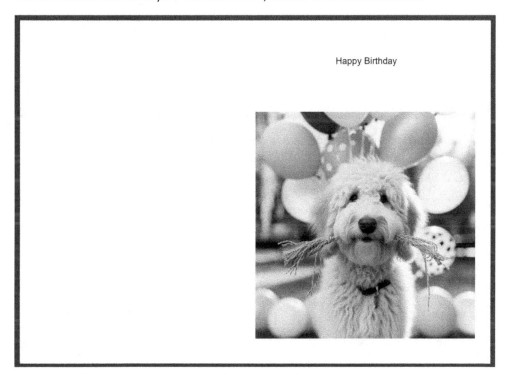

When you run the application, it will display a window within which you can select the occasion and then describe the three images you desire, as shown in Figure 11.1.

Figure 11.1: Running the CardMaker application.

Before you can run the program, you need to use pip to install the fpdf package:

C:\AIKids> pip install fpdf <Enter>

The following code implements CardMaker.py. You can download the program from my Web site at **http://www.class-files.com/CardMaker.html**.

```
import tkinter as tk
from tkinter import ttk, scrolledtext
from PIL import Image, ImageTk
from openai import OpenAI
import os
import requests

api_key = os.getenv('OpenAI_API_Key')

# Set your OpenAI API key here
client = OpenAI(api_key = api_key)

page2_verse = ""
page3_verse = ""
Heading = ""

def create_card():
  global page2_verse, page3_verse, Heading

  image1 = image1_desc_entry.get('1.0', 'end-1c')
  image2 = image2_desc_entry.get('1.0', 'end-1c')
  image3 = image3_desc_entry.get('1.0', 'end-1c')

  if image1 and image2 and image3:
   create_card_button.config(state=tk.DISABLED)  # Disable the button
   close_button.config(state=tk.DISABLED)  # Disable the button

  selected_option = choice.get()

  if selected_option == "Option 1":
    Heading = "Happy Birthday"
    MainDescription = "Write an 8 line birthday poem"
    SecondDescription = "Write a four-line poem with best wishes"
  elif selected_option == "Option 2":
    Heading = "Happy Graduation"
    MainDescription = "Write an 8 line graduation poem"
```

```
      SecondDescription = "Write a four-line poem with best wishes"
   elif selected_option == "Option 3":
      Heading = "Love"
      MainDescription = "Write an 8 line love poem"
      SecondDescription = "Write a four-line poem about love"
   elif selected_option == "Option 4":
      Heading = "Happy Thanksgiving"
      MainDescription = "Write an 8 line thanksgiving poem"
      SecondDescription = "Write a four-line poem about family"
   elif selected_option == "Option 5":
      Heading = "Merry Christmas"
      MainDescription = "Write an 8 line Christmas poem"
      SecondDescription = "Write a four-line poem about Christmas wishes"
   elif selected_option == "Option 6":
      Heading = "With Sympathy"
      MainDescription = "Write an 8 line sympathy poem"
      SecondDescription = "Write a four-line poem about life"

   output_entry.delete('1.0', 'end-1c')
   output_entry.insert('1.0', "Processing ... may take some time ...")

   image_description = image1_desc_entry.get('1.0', 'end-1c')

   # Call the ChatGPT model
   response = client.images.generate(
    model="dall-e-3",
    prompt=image_description,
    size="1024x1024",
    quality="standard",
    n=1,)

   image_response = requests.get(response.data[0].url)
   if image_response.status_code == 200:
      with open("image1.png", 'wb') as f:
        f.write(image_response.content)
        f.close()

   output_entry.delete('1.0', 'end-1c')
   output_entry.insert('1.0', "Still Processing...")

   image_description = image2_desc_entry.get('1.0', 'end-1c')
```

```python
# Call the ChatGPT model
response = client.images.generate(
 model="dall-e-3",
 prompt=image_description,
 size="1024x1024",
 quality="standard",
 n=1,)

image_response = requests.get(response.data[0].url)
if image_response.status_code == 200:
  with open("image2.png", 'wb') as f:
    f.write(image_response.content)
    f.close()

output_entry.delete('1.0', 'end-1c')
output_entry.insert('1.0', "Processing ... may take some time ...")

image_description = image3_desc_entry.get('1.0', 'end-1c')

# Call the ChatGPT model
response = client.images.generate(
 model="dall-e-3",
 prompt=image_description,
 size="1024x1024",
 quality="standard",
 n=1,)

image_response = requests.get(response.data[0].url)
if image_response.status_code == 200:
  with open("image3.png", 'wb') as f:
    f.write(image_response.content)
    f.close()

output_entry.delete('1.0', 'end-1c')
output_entry.insert('1.0', "Still Processing ... ")

# Call the ChatGPT model
response = client.chat.completions.create(
 model="gpt-4",
 messages=[
  {"role": "assistant", "content": "limit each line to 7 words or less" },
```

```
        {"role": "assistant", "content": "Do not include single or double quote
marks in the text" },
        {"role": "assistant", "content": "Do not include an apostrophe in the text"
},
        {"role": "user", "content": MainDescription}
      ]
    )

    page2_verse = response.choices[0].message.content

    output_entry.delete('1.0', 'end-1c')
    output_entry.insert('1.0', "Processing ... may take some time ...")

    # Call the ChatGPT model
    response = client.chat.completions.create(
      model="gpt-4",
      messages=[
        {"role": "assistant", "content": "limit each line to 7 words or less" },
        {"role": "assistant", "content": "Do not include single or double quote
marks in the text" },
        {"role": "assistant", "content": "Do not include an apostrophe in the text"
},
        {"role": "user", "content": SecondDescription}
      ]
    )

    page3_verse = response.choices[0].message.content

    create_PDF()
    output_entry.delete('1.0', 'end-1c')
    output_entry.insert('1.0', "Created the PDF: MyCard.pdf")

    create_card_button.config(state=tk.NORMAL)  # Enable the button
    close_button.config(state=tk.NORMAL)  # Enable the button
  else:
    output_entry.delete('1.0', 'end-1c')
    output_entry.insert('1.0', "You must describe all three images")

from fpdf import FPDF

def create_PDF():
  global page2_verse, page3_verse, Heading
```

```python
# Create a PDF object
pdf = FPDF(orientation='L')  # Set orientation to landscape

# Add a page
pdf.add_page()
pdf.set_font("Arial", size=16)
pdf.set_xy(pdf.w / 2, 20)  # Set position at the top of the right half
pdf.cell(0, 10, Heading, 0, 2, 'C')  # Center-aligned text

img_width = pdf.w
img_height = pdf.h

# Calculate resizing to fit on the right-hand side
page_width = pdf.w - 20  # Adjust for margins
if img_width > page_width / 2:  # Ensure image fits on the right side
    ratio = (page_width / 2) / img_width
    img_width *= ratio
    img_height *= ratio

# Calculate position for the image on the right-hand side
img_x = pdf.w - img_width - 10
img_y = (pdf.h - img_height) / 2

# Draw resized image1.png on the right-hand side of the first page
pdf.image("image1.png", x=img_x, y=img_y, w=img_width)

# Add a new page
pdf.add_page()

# Second Page
# Get image dimensions to calculate the resizing for image2.png
img_width2 = pdf.w / 3
img_height2 = pdf.h / 3

# Draw resized image2.png to fill the top half of the second page
pdf.image("image2.png", x=30, y=10, h=img_height2, w=img_width2)

# Get image dimensions to calculate the resizing for image3.png
# (to fill bottom right half of page 2)
img_width3 = pdf.w / 2
img_height3 = pdf.h / 2
```

```python
    # Draw resized image3.png to fill the bottom right half of the second page
    pdf.image("image3.png", x=pdf.w/2, y=pdf.h / 2 - 10, w=img_width3)

    pdf.set_font("Arial", size=10)
    pdf.set_xy(10, img_height2 + 20)

    # Manually set line height (distance between lines)
    line_height = 12  # Adjust this value to set the desired line spacing

    # Split text by newline character
    lines = page2_verse.split('\n')

    for line in lines:
        if line != '\n\n':
            pdf.cell(0, line_height, txt=line, ln=True)

    # Split text by newline character
    lines = page3_verse.split('\n')

    i = 30
    for line in lines:
        pdf.set_xy(pdf.w/2 + 10, i)
        pdf.cell(0, line_height, txt=line, ln=True)
        i = i + 10

    # Save the PDF
    pdf.output("MyCard.pdf")

def close_window():
    root.destroy()

import threading

def call_api_in_thread():
    # Function to call the API in a separate thread
    thread = threading.Thread(target=create_card)
    thread.start()

root = tk.Tk()
root.title("Card Maker")

# Maximize the window
```

```
root.attributes('-fullscreen', True)  # For Linux systems

# Create a Canvas widget with a vertical scrollbar
canvas = tk.Canvas(root)
canvas.pack(side=tk.LEFT, fill=tk.BOTH, expand=True)

scrollbar = ttk.Scrollbar(root, orient=tk.VERTICAL, command=canvas.yview)
scrollbar.pack(side=tk.RIGHT, fill=tk.Y)
canvas.configure(yscrollcommand=scrollbar.set)

# Create a Frame within the canvas to hold all the widgets
main_frame = tk.Frame(canvas)
main_frame.pack(fill=tk.BOTH, expand=True)

canvas.create_window((0, 0), window=main_frame, anchor=tk.NW)

choice = tk.StringVar()

option1 = tk.Radiobutton(main_frame, text="Birthday", variable=choice,
value="Option 1")
option1.grid(row=2, column=0, padx=10, pady=3)

option2 = tk.Radiobutton(main_frame, text="Graduation", variable=choice,
value="Option 2")
option2.grid(row=2, column=1, padx=10, pady=3)

option3 = tk.Radiobutton(main_frame, text="Love", variable=choice,
value="Option 3")
option3.grid(row=2, column=2, padx=10, pady=3)

option4 = tk.Radiobutton(main_frame, text="Thanksgiving", variable=choice,
value="Option 4")
option4.grid(row=3, column=0, padx=10, pady=3)

option5 = tk.Radiobutton(main_frame, text="Christmas", variable=choice,
value="Option 5")
option5.grid(row=3, column=1, padx=10, pady=3)

option6 = tk.Radiobutton(main_frame, text="Sympathy", variable=choice,
value="Option 6")
option6.grid(row=3, column=2, padx=10, pady=3)
```

```python
choice.set("Option 1")

# Image Description Label and Entry
image1_desc_label = tk.Label(main_frame, text="Page 1 Image Description:")
image1_desc_label.grid(row=4, column=0, padx=10, pady=5)

image1_desc_entry = tk.Text(main_frame, height=5, width=80)
image1_desc_entry.grid(row=4, column=1, padx=10, pady=5)

image2_desc_label = tk.Label(main_frame, text="Page 2 Image Description:")
image2_desc_label.grid(row=5, column=0, padx=10, pady=5)

image2_desc_entry = tk.Text(main_frame, height=5, width=80)
image2_desc_entry.grid(row=5, column=1, padx=10, pady=5)

image3_desc_label = tk.Label(main_frame, text="Page 3 Image Description:")
image3_desc_label.grid(row=9, column=0, padx=10, pady=5)

image3_desc_entry = tk.Text(main_frame, height=5, width=80)
image3_desc_entry.grid(row=9, column=1, padx=10, pady=5)

output_label = tk.Label(main_frame, text="Output Status:")
output_label.grid(row=10, column=0, padx=10, pady=5)

output_entry = tk.Text(main_frame, height=5, width=80)
output_entry.grid(row=10, column=1, padx=10, pady=5)

create_card_button = tk.Button(main_frame, text="Generate Card",
command=call_api_in_thread)
create_card_button.grid(row=13, column=0, padx=10, pady=5)

# Close Button
close_button = tk.Button(main_frame, text="Close", command=close_window)
close_button.grid(row=13, column=2, padx=10, pady=5)

# Update the canvas scroll region
main_frame.update_idletasks()  # Ensure all widgets are displayed properly
canvas.config(scrollregion=canvas.bbox(tk.ALL))

root.mainloop()
```

Let's understand the code. To start, the create_card function does most of the work. It first checks to make sure the user has described all three of the card images. Then, the function disables the two buttons, so the user does not click them while the function is performing its processing.

Next, the function calls the OpenAI three times to produce card images based on the three descriptions. Then, the function calls the OpenAI to generate two poems, one for the card's page 2 and one for page 3. Finally, the function calls the create_PDF function and re-enables the buttons.

The create_PDF function will print the images created by the create_card function: image1.png, image2.png, and image3.png. To create a card, the function will create a PDF in landscape orientation. The create_PDF function begins by sizing image1.png so it will fit in the bottom right corner of page one. At the top of the page, the function prints Happy Birthday, Merry Christmas, and so on based on the radio button the user originally chose within the CardMaker application.

Next, the create_PDF function will layout the inside of the card (page 2 of the PDF). The function reduces image2.png to 1/3 of the size of the page and displays it in the upper-left corner of the page. The function reduces image3.png to fit in the lower-right corner of the page. Then, the function displays the text for the 8-line poem beneath the small image and the text for the 4-line poem above the large image, completing the card.

If you examine the OpenAI API calls that generate the poems, you will find that each uses assistant messages to provide directives to the API about the specific poems to create. In this way, the application can ensure the poem text OpenAI generates will fit correctly within the PDF locations. In addition, the messages reduce the chance of the text containing quote characters which the PDF software was having difficulty displaying correctly.

When your programs call the OpenAI AI to create a card, OpenAI may take some time to generate the result. When we call OpenAI from a script that uses tkinter to display a window, this delay can cause problems with our user interface. To eliminate these problems, we'll create a second thread in our script that asks OpenAI to generate the text, while our program's main thread continues to manage our user interface. To create the second thread, we'll use Python's threading package (which we import) and we'll create a second thread to call our create_card function which interacts with OpenAI:

import threading

```
def call_api_in_thread():
    # Function to call the API in a separate thread
    thread = threading.Thread(target=create_card)
    thread.start()
```

Finally, the rest of our code creates the original user interface that lets the user specify the text they desire.

When the user clicks the Generate Card button, the code will call our function call_api_in_thread which, in turn, calls OpenAI:

```
create_card_button = tk.Button(main_frame, text="Generate Card",
command=call_api_in_thread)
create_card_button.grid(row=13, column=0, padx=10, pady=5)
```

Summary

In this chapter, you used OpenAI to transcribe an audio file to text using natural-language processing. In the next chapter, you will use OpenAI to create an animated GIF which contains the four images you specify.

Chapter 12
Coding an AI GIF Animator

We live in a world of memes with millions sent daily by text. In this chapter, you will create a program that uses AI to generate an animated GIF based on four images you describe.

Generate Animated GIF	— ☐ ✕
Image 1 Description	A cream-colored labradoodle in a library looking for books.
Image 2 Description	A cream-colored labradoodle in a library picking a book.
Image 3 Description	A cream-colored labradoodle in a library reading a book in a chair.
Image 4 Description	A cream-colored labradoodle sound asleep in the chair.
Output:	Animated GIF Created.
	Generate GIF

To run the program, use the following Python command:

C:\AIKids> python GIFMaker.py <Enter>

When the script completes, it will create a file in your current folder named animated.gif. The following code implements GIFMaker.py. You can download the code from my Web site at **http://www.class-files.com/GIFMaker.html**.

```
from PIL import Image, ImageSequence
import tkinter as tk
from openai import OpenAI
import os
import requests

api_key = os.getenv('OpenAI_API_Key')

# Set your OpenAI API key here
client = OpenAI(api_key = api_key)

def create_animated_gif():
  generate_gif_button.config(state=tk.DISABLED)

  image_descriptions = [
    image1_description.get(1.0, tk.END),
    image2_description.get(1.0, tk.END),
    image3_description.get(1.0, tk.END),
    image4_description.get(1.0, tk.END)
  ]

  images = []

  image_paths = ["image1.png", "image2.png", "image3.png", "image4.png"]
  i = 0
  output_text.delete(1.0, tk.END)  # Clear any existing text
  output_text.insert(tk.END, "Processing...")

  for description in image_descriptions:
   if len(description) == 1:
    output_text.delete(1.0, tk.END)  # Clear any existing text
    output_text.insert(tk.END, "Must specify description for each image.")
    generate_gif_button.config(state=tk.NORMAL)
    return
```

```python
  # Call the ChatGPT model
  response = client.images.generate(
    model="dall-e-3",
    prompt=description,
    size="1024x1024",
    quality="standard",
    n=1,)

  image_response = requests.get(response.data[0].url)
  if image_response.status_code == 200:
    with open(image_paths[i], 'wb') as f:
      f.write(image_response.content)
      f.close()

  image = Image.open(image_paths[i])
  image.thumbnail((512, 512))  # Resize the image
  images.append(image)
  i = i + 1

  # Save images as an animated GIF with a frame duration of 2000
milliseconds
  images[0].save("animated.gif", save_all=True, append_images=images[1:],
    optimize=False, duration=2000, loop=0)
  output_text.delete(1.0, tk.END)  # Clear any existing text
  output_text.insert(tk.END, "Animated GIF Created.")
  generate_gif_button.config(state=tk.NORMAL)

import threading

def call_api_in_thread():
  # Function to call the API in a separate thread
  thread = threading.Thread(target=create_animated_gif)
  thread.start()

root = tk.Tk()
root.title("Generate Animated GIF")

# Create and place text boxes for image descriptions
image1_description_label = tk.Label(root, text="Image 1 Description")
image1_description_label.grid(row=0, column=0)
image1_description = tk.Text(root, height=4, width=80)
image1_description.grid(row=0, column=1)
```

```
image2_description_label = tk.Label(root, text="Image 2 Description")
image2_description_label.grid(row=1, column=0)
image2_description = tk.Text(root, height=4, width=80)
image2_description.grid(row=1, column=1)

image3_description_label = tk.Label(root, text="Image 3 Description")
image3_description_label.grid(row=2, column=0)
image3_description = tk.Text(root, height=4, width=80)
image3_description.grid(row=2, column=1)

image4_description_label = tk.Label(root, text="Image 4 Description")
image4_description_label.grid(row=3, column=0)
image4_description = tk.Text(root, height=4, width=80)
image4_description.grid(row=3, column=1)

output_text_label = tk.Label(root, text="Output:")
output_text_label.grid(row=4, column=0)
output_text = tk.Text(root, height=4, width=80)
output_text.grid(row=4, column=1)

# Create a button to generate the animated GIF
generate_gif_button = tk.Button(root, text="Generate GIF",
command=call_api_in_thread)
generate_gif_button.grid(row=5, columnspan=2)

image_label = tk.Label(root)
image_label.grid(row=6, column=0)

root.mainloop()
```

Let's understand the code. The first few lines import the needed Python packages and provide your OpenAI API key to OpenAI:

```
import tkinter as tk
from tkinter import scrolledtext
from PIL import Image, ImageTk
from fpdf import FPDF  # For creating PDF
from openai import OpenAI
import os
import requests
```

```
api_key = os.getenv('OpenAI_API_Key')

# Set your OpenAI API key here
client = OpenAI(api_key = api_key)
```

After the user types the image descriptions and clicks the Generate GIF button, the code calls the create_animated_gif function which does much of the work. The function uses an if statement to check that the user has specified descriptions for each image. If the user has not, the function displays an error message in the output box.

```
def create_animated_gif():
  image_descriptions = [
    image1_description.get(1.0, tk.END),
    image2_description.get(1.0, tk.END),
    image3_description.get(1.0, tk.END),
    image4_description.get(1.0, tk.END)
  ]

  images = []

  image_paths = ["image1.png", "image2.png", "image3.png", "image4.png"]
  i = 0
  output_text.delete(1.0, tk.END)  # Clear any existing text
  output_text.insert(tk.END, "Processing...")

  for description in image_descriptions:
   if len(description) == 1:
    output_text.delete(1.0, tk.END)  # Clear any existing text
    output_text.insert(tk.END, "Must specify description for each image.")
    return

  # Call the ChatGPT model
  response = client.images.generate(
   model="dall-e-3",
   prompt=description,
   size="1024x1024",
   quality="standard",
   n=1,)

  image_response = requests.get(response.data[0].url)
  if image_response.status_code == 200:
```

```
        with open(image_paths[i], 'wb') as f:
          f.write(image_response.content)
          f.close()

     image = Image.open(image_paths[i])
     image.thumbnail((512, 512))  # Resize the image
     images.append(image)
     i = i + 1

  # Save images as an animated GIF with a frame duration of 2000
milliseconds
  images[0].save("animated.gif", save_all=True, append_images=images[1:],
     optimize=False, duration=2000, loop=0)
  output_text.delete(1.0, tk.END)  # Clear any existing text
  output_text.insert(tk.END, "Animated GIF Created.")
```

Next, for each image, the function calls the OpenAI API to generate an image from the description, saving the images as Image1.png, Image2.png, Image3.png, and Image4.png. The code resizes each image and then assigns them to the animated GIF image with a duration of 2 seconds per frame.

As discussed, OpenAI may take some time to create the image and generate the recipe. When we call OpenAI from a script that uses tkinter to display a window, this delay can cause problems with our user interface. To eliminate these problems, we'll create a second thread in our script that asks OpenAI the question, while our program's main thread continues to manage our user interface. To create the second thread, we'll use Python's threading package (which we import) and we'll create a second thread to call our create_animated_gif function which interacts with OpenAI:

```
import threading

def call_api_in_thread():
  # Function to call the API in a separate thread
  thread = threading.Thread(target=create_animated_gif)
  thread.start()
```

Finally, the rest of our code creates our text boxes and button.

Summary

In this chapter, you used OpenAI to generate images based on your descriptions and your program then combined the images into an animated GIF. In the next chapter, you will learn to use OpenAI to perform natural-language processing by generating speech from text.

Chapter 13
Using AI to Generate Speech from Text

Natural-language processing is a subset of artificial intelligence that focuses on a computer program's ability to interpret, understand, and generate human speech in much the same way that the human brain does. In this chapter, you will get started with natural-language processing by using AI to generate speech from text.

Creating Quick Speech Generation with Your Own Program

Using natural-language processing, your programs can convert speech from written text. The following Python script, SimpleSpeech.py, uses the OpenAI API to generate an audio file from a text description. To run the script, you can use the AIKids Jupyter Notebook or you can create and run the script from the Anaconda prompt:

C:\AIKids> python SimpleSpeech.py <Enter>

After the program runs, it will create the file Speech.mp3 in your current folder. If you double-click on the file using the Windows Explorer, Windows will play the audio file. The following script creates SimpleSpeech.py. You can download the program from my Web site at **http://www.class-files.com/SimpleSpeech.html**.

```
import os
from openai import OpenAI

key = os.getenv('OpenAI_API_Key')

# Set your OpenAI API key here
client = OpenAI(api_key = key)

speech_file_path =  "speech.mp3"
response = client.audio.speech.create(
  model="tts-1",
  voice="alloy",
  input="Hello, OpenAI World. This is your first text to speech application!"
```

```
)
```

response.stream_to_file(speech_file_path)

Let's understand the code. The first four lines import the Python packages and script requires and then gets your OpenAP API key and prepares OpenAI for use. Then, the script calls the OpenAI API telling it to use the tts-1 model and the alloy voice. The API call specifies the text you want the API to generate to speech.

Take time to experiment with the script by changing the text that it uses to generate speech.

Asking the User for the Speech to Generate

The previous script worked—it generated speech. But, each time you want to generate new speech, you had to edit and save the program. A better program will ask the user to specify the text they want to convert to speech. You can do so using the Python input function. You can download the AskSpeech.py program from my Web site at **http://www.class-files.com/AskSpeech.html**.

```python
import os
from openai import OpenAI

key = os.getenv('OpenAI_API_Key')

# Set your OpenAI API key here
client = OpenAI(api_key = key)

text = input("Type the text you want to convert to speech: ")

speech_file_path = "speech.mp3"
response = client.audio.speech.create(
  model="tts-1",
  voice="onyx",
  input=text
)

response.stream_to_file(speech_file_path)
```

To run the script, use Python as follows:

C:\AIKids> python AskSpeech.py <Enter>
Type the text you want to convert to speech: This is a test!

Again, the script will create a file named Speech.mp3 in your current folder. The script processing is very similar to the first script with the exception that it uses the input function to prompt the user for the text to convert and then passes that script to the OpenAI API. The API call uses a different voice, onyx to generate the speech.

Creating a Fancy Speech-Generation Program

The previous two speech-generation programs created speech from the desired text. The second program, AskSpeech.py, improved on the first by using the input function to get the desired text from the user. The following Python script, Speech.py, creates a fancier user interface, similar to that shown in Figure 13.1.

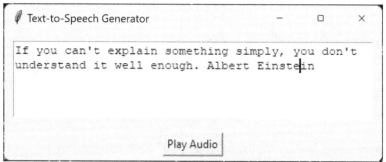

Figure 13.1: A fancy user interface for generating speech.

The following script implements Speech.py. You can download the program from my Web site at **http://www.class-files.com/Speech.html**.

```python
import tkinter as tk
import os
from openai import OpenAI
import pygame

# Set your OpenAI API key here
key = os.getenv('OpenAI_API_Key')
client = OpenAI(api_key=key)

def generate_and_play_audio():
    play_button.config(state=tk.DISABLED)  # Disable the button

    text = text_entry.get("1.0", tk.END).strip()  # Get text from the text box
```

```
      pygame.mixer.quit()
      pygame.quit()

   if text:
      try:
         # Generate speech from the text using OpenAI
         speech_file_path = "speech.mp3"
         response = client.audio.speech.create(
            model="tts-1",
            voice="nova",
            input=text
         )
         response.stream_to_file(speech_file_path)

         # Play the generated audio
         pygame.init()
         pygame.mixer.init()
         pygame.mixer.music.load(speech_file_path)
         pygame.mixer.music.play()

      except Exception as e:
         print(f"Error: {e}")

      play_button.config(state=tk.NORMAL)  # Enable the button

import threading

def call_api_in_thread():
   # Function to call the API in a separate thread
   thread = threading.Thread(target=generate_and_play_audio)
   thread.start()

# Create a Tkinter window
root = tk.Tk()
root.title("Text-to-Speech Generator")

# Create a text box for entering text
text_entry = tk.Text(root, height=5, width=50)
text_entry.pack(padx=10, pady=10)

# Create a button to play audio
```

```
play_button = tk.Button(root, text="Play Audio",
command=call_api_in_thread)
play_button.pack(padx=10, pady=5)

# Start the Tkinter event loop
root.mainloop()
```

Let's understand the code. The first few lines import the Python packages the code requires, gets your OpenAI API key, and prepares OpenAI for use:

```
import tkinter as tk
import os
from openai import OpenAI
import pygame

# Set your OpenAI API key here
key = os.getenv('OpenAI_API_Key')
client = OpenAI(api_key=key)
```

The generate_and_play_audio function does most of the work. The function first disables the Play Audio button so the user cannot click it while the OpenAI is generating speech. Then, the function gets the desired text from the text box. The function then quits the pygame audio software in case it was previously open to avoid an error that the script can't save the audio to the speech.mp3 file because it was previously open.

Next, the function calls the OpenAPI API to generate the speech. When the API completes, the function saves the audio to the file speech.mp3 in your current folder. The script then uses pygame to play the audio file. Lastly, the function re-enables the Play Audio file.

```
def generate_and_play_audio():
    play_button.config(state=tk.DISABLED)  # Disable the button

    text = text_entry.get("1.0", tk.END).strip()  # Get text from the text box
    pygame.mixer.quit()
    pygame.quit()

    if text:
        try:
            # Generate speech from the text using OpenAI
            speech_file_path = "speech.mp3"
            response = client.audio.speech.create(
```

```
        model="tts-1",
        voice="nova",
        input=text
    )
    response.stream_to_file(speech_file_path)

    # Play the generated audio
    pygame.init()
    pygame.mixer.init()
    pygame.mixer.music.load(speech_file_path)
    pygame.mixer.music.play()

except Exception as e:
    print(f"Error: {e}")


play_button.config(state=tk.NORMAL)  # Enable the button
```

When your programs call the OpenAI AI to generate text (or images and speech) OpenAI may take some time to generate the result. When we call OpenAI from a script that uses tkinter to display a window, this delay can cause problems with our user interface. To eliminate these problems, we'll create a second thread in our script that asks OpenAI to generate the text, while our program's main thread continues to manage our user interface. To create the second thread, we'll use Python's threading package (which we import) and we'll create a second thread to call our generate_and_play_audio function which interacts with OpenAI:

```
import threading

def call_api_in_thread():
    # Function to call the API in a separate thread
    thread = threading.Thread(target=generate_and_play_audio)
    thread.start()
```

Finally, the rest of our code creates the original user interface that lets the user specify the text they desire.

When the user clicks the Play Audio button, the code will call our function call_api_in_thread which, in turn, calls OpenAI:

```
play_button = tk.Button(root, text="Play Audio",
command=call_api_in_thread)
play_button.pack(padx=10, pady=5)
```

Summary

In this chapter, you used OpenAI to generate speech based on the text you specify. In the next chapter, you will learn to use OpenAI to perform additional natural-language processing by transcribing audio to text.

Chapter 14
Transcribing Speech to Text

You have learned that natural-language processing is a subset of artificial intelligence that focuses on a computer program's ability to interpret, understand, and generate human speech in much the same way that the human brain does. In Chapter 13, you learned to generate speech from text. In this chapter, you will do just the opposite—you will transcribe audio into text.

Creating Quick Speech Transcriber with Your Own Program

Using natural-language processing, your programs can convert speech from written text. Likewise, you can also transcribe speech to text. The following Python script, SimpleTranscriber.py, uses the OpenAI API to produce text from the speech an audio file contains. To run the script, you can use the AIKids Jupyter Notebook or you can create and run the script from the Anaconda prompt:

C:\AIKids> python SimpleTranscriber.py <Enter>

When the script runs, it will open the file Speech.mp3 from your current folder and display the text that corresponds to the audio. The following script creates SimpleTranscriber.py. You can download the program from my Web site at **http://www.class-files.com/SimpleTranscriber.html**.

```
from openai import OpenAI
import os

key = os.getenv('OpenAI_API_Key')

# Set your OpenAI API key here
client = OpenAI(api_key = key)

audio = open("speech.mp3", 'rb')
transcript = client.audio.transcriptions.create(
   model="whisper-1",
   file=audio
 )
```

print(transcript.text)

Let's understand the code. The first four lines import the Python packages and script requires and then gets your OpenAP API key and prepares OpenAI for use. Then, the script calls the OpenAI API telling it to use to the whisper-1 model to transcribe the audio file speech.mp3 to text. When the API completes, the script displays the transcription text.

Take time to experiment with the script by changing the audio file that it uses to generate speech.

Asking the User for the File to Transcribe

The previous script worked—it transcribed speech. But, each time you wanted to transcribe a different audio, you had to edit and save the program. A better program will ask the user to specify the file they want to transcribe. You can do so using the Python input function. You can download the AskSpeech.py program from my Web site at **http://www.class-files.com/AskSpeech.html**.

```
from openai import OpenAI
import os

key = os.getenv('OpenAI_API_Key')

# Set your OpenAI API key here
client = OpenAI(api_key = key)

audio_file = input("Type the name of the file to transcribe: ")

audio = open("speech.mp3", 'rb')
transcript = client.audio.transcriptions.create(
    model="whisper-1",
    file=audio
)
```

print(transcript.text)

To run the script, use Python as follows:

```
C:\AIKids> python AskTranscribe.py   <Enter>
Type the name of the file to transcribe: myaudio.mp3
```

Again, the script will open and describe an audio file. The script processing is very similar to the first script with the exception that it uses the input function to prompt the user for the file to transcribe and then passes that script to the OpenAI API.

Creating a Fancy Speech-Transcription Program

The previous two speech-transcription programs transcribe speech and generated the desired text. The second program, AskTranscriber.py, improved on the first by using the input function to get the desired audio file from the user. The following Python script, Transcribe.py, creates a fancier user interface, similar to that shown in Figure 14.1.

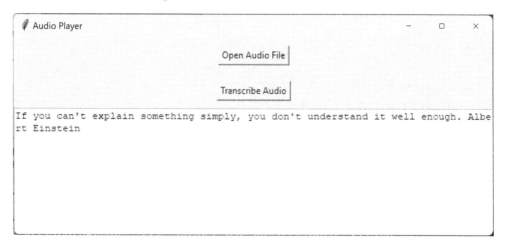

Figure 14.1: A fancy user interface for transcribing speech.

The following script implements Transcribe.py. You can download the program from my Web site at **http://www.class-files.com/Transcribe.html**.

```
import tkinter as tk
from tkinter import filedialog
from openai import OpenAI
import os

# Set your OpenAI API key here
key = os.getenv('OpenAI_API_Key')
client = OpenAI(api_key=key)

def open_audio_file():
    file_path = filedialog.askopenfilename(filetypes=[("Audio Files",
"*.mp3;*.wav;*.ogg")])
```

```
    if file_path:
        entry_audio_file.delete(1.0, tk.END)
        entry_audio_file.insert(1.0, file_path)

def transcribe_audio():
    button_open_audio.config(state=tk.DISABLED)  # Disable the button
    button_transcribe_audio.config(state=tk.DISABLED)  # Disable the button

    audio_file = entry_audio_file.get(1.0, tk.END).strip()

    audio = open(audio_file, 'rb')
    transcript = client.audio.transcriptions.create(
        model="whisper-1",
        file=audio
    )

    entry_audio_file.delete(1.0, tk.END)
    entry_audio_file.insert(1.0, transcript.text)
    button_open_audio.config(state=tk.NORMAL)  # Enable the button
    button_transcribe_audio.config(state=tk.NORMAL)  # Enable the button

import threading

def call_api_in_thread():
    # Function to call the API in a separate thread
    thread = threading.Thread(target=transcribe_audio)
    thread.start()

root = tk.Tk()
root.title("Audio Player")

# Function buttons
button_open_audio = tk.Button(root, text="Open Audio File",
command=open_audio_file)
button_open_audio.pack(pady=10)

button_transcribe_audio = tk.Button(root, text="Transcribe Audio",
command=call_api_in_thread)
button_transcribe_audio.pack(pady=10)

# Text box to display the selected audio file or message
entry_audio_file = tk.Text(root, height=10, width=80)
```

```
entry_audio_file.pack()

root.mainloop()
```

Let's understand the code. The first few lines import the Python packages the code requires, gets your OpenAI API key, and prepares OpenAI for use:

```
import tkinter as tk
from tkinter import filedialog
from openai import OpenAI
import os

# Set your OpenAI API key here
key = os.getenv('OpenAI_API_Key')
client = OpenAI(api_key=key)
```

The play_audio function does most of the work. The function first disables the Transcribe Audio and Open Audio File buttons so the user cannot click them while the OpenAI is transcribing speech. Then, the function gets the desired file from the text box.

Next, the function calls the OpenAPI API to transcribe the speech. When the API completes, the function displays the text in the text box. Lastly, the function re-enables the Play Transcribe Audio and Open File buttons.

```
def transcribe_audio():
  button_open_audio.config(state=tk.DISABLED)  # Disable the button
  button_transcribe_audio.config(state=tk.DISABLED)  # Disable the button

  audio_file = entry_audio_file.get(1.0, tk.END).strip()

  audio = open(audio_file, 'rb')
  transcript = client.audio.transcriptions.create(
    model="whisper-1",
    file=audio
  )

  entry_audio_file.delete(1.0, tk.END)
  entry_audio_file.insert(1.0, transcript.text)
  button_open_audio.config(state=tk.NORMAL)  # Enable the button
  button_transcribe_audio.config(state=tk.NORMAL)  # Enable the button
```

When your programs call the OpenAI AI to transcribe audio, OpenAI may take some time to generate the result. When we call OpenAI from a script that uses tkinter to display a window, this delay can cause problems with our user interface. To eliminate these problems, we'll create a second thread in our script that asks OpenAI to generate the text, while our program's main thread continues to manage our user interface. To create the second thread, we'll use Python's threading package (which we import) and we'll create a second thread to call our transcribe_audio function which interacts with OpenAI:

import threading

```
def call_api_in_thread():
    # Function to call the API in a separate thread
    thread = threading.Thread(target=transcribe_audio)
    thread.start()
```

Finally, the rest of our code creates the original user interface that lets the user specify the text they desire.

When the user clicks the Transcribe Audio button, the code will call our function call_api_in_thread which, in turn, calls OpenAI:

```
button_transcribe_audio = tk.Button(root, text="Transcribe Audio",
command=call_api_in_thread)
```

Summary

In this chapter, you used OpenAI to transcribe an audio file to text using natural-language processing. Congratulations. By now you have a strong understanding of the processing OpenAI performs. You should take time now to experiment with and change the applications this book presents to better understand their processing.

Learning More About AI Programming on YouTube

To help you learn more about AI programming, I have created a YouTube channel that is filled with programming videos. You can find the channel at **https://www.youtube.com/@krisjamsa6753** as shown in Figure 1. Take time now to check out the videos and to learn more AI programming.

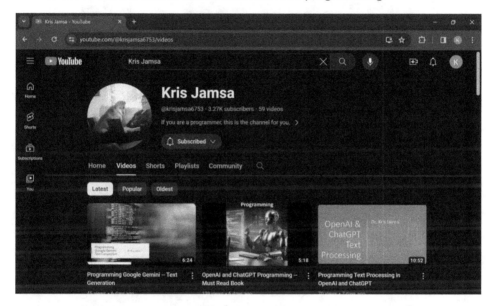

Figure 1: My YouTube channel.

Available Now on Amazon

Continuing learning more about OpenAI and ChatGPT programming. The book contains 50 real-world applications with the complete Python code.

Index

www.ingramcontent.com/pod-product-compliance
Lightning Source LLC
LaVergne TN
LVHW081344050326
832903LV00024B/1305